The Softer Side of Single

AMY H. SMITH

To Dad and Mom,
for being living examples of what a true husband/father and wife/mother are supposed to look like, and for teaching me what True Love is (and isn't).

To my sister, Staci,
for always being my best friend and unconditional supporter.

To my grandparents,
Edward and Norma Harrell and Melvin and Evangeline West, for showing us all the beauty of marriage the way God intended it, and for modeling the real meaning of "'til death do us part."

To my *the one* and to our future and family together,
I love you with all my heart;
I always have, and I always will.

CONTENTS

Introduction
A NEW PERSPECTIVE

I went to work that day reluctantly. My heart felt like it had been completely crushed, my mind was whirling in a million directions, and I could cry without a moment's notice. I had never been dumped before, and it felt horrible. But it wasn't just about being dumped. For the past seven months, he and I had been talking about wedding plans, convinced that God had brought us together and that we were *the one* for each other. This wasn't just about a breakup. This also meant that when it came to what I thought was God's will for my life, I was wrong. Again. This went beyond the emotional, although the emotion was no lighthearted matter. This shook me to my spiritual core.

> *God, how do I keep missing You on this? How will I ever know it's Your voice, when I've been wrong about Your voice now so many times? Why do I keep giving my heart to men who don't want it or don't deserve it? How do I keep my focus on You and not allow a guy to steal it away? And in all of this, what do I do with this longing I have for a husband ... and how long do I have to live with it unfulfilled?*

The breakup had happened the night before over the phone. I couldn't believe that after all the promises he had made to me, he was so nonchalant and stoic about calling it quits and walking away. We had just been planning the rest of our lives together, and now I don't matter anymore? He had said he knew God wanted us together. Did God change His mind?

This sense of betrayal and abandonment was new to me. Of course, the hurt and heartache were expected. However, even in the middle of processing all these thoughts and feelings, what I didn't expect was the mixture of a completely different emotion I began feeling almost immediately... Was it normal to be feeling this the day after a breakup? While still reeling and freshly mourning the loss of the relationship, the shattered dreams, the broken promises, I felt this very strange but very welcome sense of... freedom.

Even through the pain, I realized that I was now free from all the weight I had been carrying throughout this relationship. I no longer had to try to convince myself daily that this was God's will. I no longer had to fight to push away that little nagging sense that something wasn't quite right about our being together. Yes, this meant I would have to start over. Yes, I was older than I wanted to be while SWNP (single with no prospects) again. But this also meant I was free to dream again! I no longer had to try to fit this person into the silhouette God had painted on my heart for my future spouse – a silhouette this guy just couldn't fill no matter how hard I had tried to make him. I no longer had to try to squish my dreams to fit into the shape that my future would have been with him. I could stop wrestling with all the pieces of this relationship that just weren't matching what I knew my future was supposed to be, and I could start re-dreaming about what (and who) God actually wanted for me.

For once, it was a relief *not* to know the face to that silhouette in my heart. That freedom felt better than any moment in the previous seven months of trying to tie myself forever to someone who was not God's best for me.

That week began a journey that I had suspected all along would be necessary, but I had desperately hoped I could bypass. It began my journey of embracing and enjoying Single. Until that point, I had been in a lifelong race to get through Single as fast as I possibly could and skip happily into Marriage. But the weight of what I had almost fallen into did not escape me. I recognized that I had been so very close to committing my entire life to the wrong person; I had almost entered into a marriage that would have undoubtedly been a bumpy, difficult road, and it would have altered my entire future. That close call in my life made me so grateful that I was spared from potentially the biggest mistake of my life, in spite of my own willingness to march blindly forward for the sake of companionship. My eyes were finally starting to open to see how grateful I should be for Single – no matter how long the season of Single would last.

Out of this season come the following pages, which reflect a medley of my personal experiences, observations I have gleaned from others' experiences, and knowledge I have gained here and there along the way.

SHARING EXPERIENCES

As I begin writing this script, I write first to all of you single, Christian women, because you and I are sure to relate to one another on many levels. However, I also write to anyone, male or female, single or married, who wants to be sure your whole heart belongs to God, so that other relationships can fall in place in a healthy way. Hopefully, you will find truths from the following pages to apply to your own life in whatever stage of life you may be.

We all bring to the table a vast array of perspectives and life experiences. I'll be sharing with painful honesty many of my own. They may be similar to yours, or they may be drastically different. In either case, I encourage you to consider our common ground: Regardless of our past or present circumstances, you and I both share experience in this place called Single. We both want God's best for our lives. We both want to navigate this season successfully, and when all is said and done, we'd really like to emerge from it whole and unscathed, right?

UNFULFILLED PURPOSES

My inspiration for writing began as this: While I, like many of you, have awaited my knight in shining armor, and while I have questioned why he seems to be so far away, I began asking myself and God, *Could it be that one of the reasons I am still single is that my singleness has not yet accomplished all it is meant to? Do I have something to offer someone else before I exit this season of my life forever?* Maybe I could offer some sense of hope and reason to you in your own season of Single, and we can navigate this thing together. This project is my attempt to do just that: to take what I have in my hand – experiences in the Single season of life – and offer it to God and to you. I pray that He will use it for His purposes and for your benefit.

As I do what I feel I've been given to do, I encourage you to seek God for what unfulfilled purposes your own journey of Single may still hold. Maybe there is someone else for you to minister to or reach out to; maybe there is a young girl in need of mentoring by a godly woman; or maybe there is some endeavor you are still to attempt before you forever exit your own season of Single.

LAUNCHING THOUGHTS

As we launch into this discussion of a topic that is so attached to our hearts, dreams, and emotions, it is important to prepare ourselves to be willing to look past our surface emotions and be able to see what really lies in our hearts. Our emotions are tricky, and if you come into this with a preconceived notion (maybe you're like I was and you're inwardly trying to convince yourself that Mr. Okay is Mr. Right when you know he really isn't), your preconceived notions will handicap your grasp of the Truth we will discuss, and you will sabotage your own growth in the process.

This subject matter is too important for us to run through it blindly; if we can get this right, we can avoid worlds of heartache and irreversible consequences for the rest of our lives. So moving forward to the chapters ahead, I encourage you to join me in exercising these three principles in our hearts and minds:

1. **Be honest with yourself, no matter how painful the truth may be.** I am about to open up my life to you with a level of vulnerability that could cause me considerable fear and discomfort. My purpose in doing so is to help you open up your own life in sheer honesty before yourself and before God. If you will not be honest about where you really are emotionally, relationally, and spiritually, you will hinder yourself from walking in a life of confidence, contentment, and

true freedom. I know, because I've been there on both sides. Please trust me: The freedom that honesty brings is well worth the temporary sting of facing the Truth!

2. **Allow yourself to reevaluate decisions and assumptions you have already made.** Making mistakes is part of life; refusing to correct them is part of foolishness. Please do not doggedly hold onto a conclusion you came to in the past if you need to honestly admit a mistake in order to extract Truth and wisdom for your future. On the flip side, do not allow condemnation over past mistakes to hold you back from your future full of hope. Your past is part of the fabric of your life; it is part of what makes you who you are. Just remember that the overall fabric is beautiful, free from shame and disgrace, distinctively marked by God's Grace.

3. **Have faith that God will meet your efforts with His Love and Grace.** If you find that you need to take any corrective action, either below the surface in your emotions and heart or very practically in your current life circumstances or present relationships, know that God is going to reward your willingness to take action by giving you the Grace you need to move forward.

The following pages are an exploration not so much of how to hurry up and "get through" Single but of how to learn who we are, love the life God has given us, and appreciate whatever season we are in. The principles we learn together will help us not only during Single but for the rest of our lives!

I pray that as we take this journey together, each of us can open our eyes to see life through a clear, untainted lens, to begin to fully understand and embrace the softer side of Single.

...I have learned the secret of being content in any and every situation...
Philippians 4:12

Chapter One
THE GIFT

Evan opened his eyes abruptly and looked around. There was a tiny bit of sunlight peeking through the curtains, so that could only mean one thing: It was finally morning! Wide awake in his superhero bunk bed, he gave a swift kick to the top bunk to jar awake his little brother, Cory, and squealed with excitement, "Get up! It's morning!" Evan jumped out of bed and ran downstairs as fast as his seven-year-old legs could carry him, with Cory not far behind. The anticipation had been mounting for weeks, and this was the moment they had been waiting for: Christmas was here!

Once the entire family was awake and assembled in the family room, Dad began handing out gifts. This had been a good year for their family, and the presents were abundant. Mom sipped coffee and snapped pictures cheerfully as Evan and Cory simultaneously unwrapped rival action figures, then matching PJs, then posters of their favorite sports teams to hang on the walls in their room. Each boy opened a new video game and several gift boxes of new clothes (about which, of course, Mom was more excited than the boys, but they humored her nonetheless). Dad and Mom took turns exchanging gifts as the boys watched, giddy with anticipation for what was still to come. They loved all their gifts so far, but they knew the big one was coming. Dad and Mom always bought each boy one very special gift for Christmas, and they always saved it for last.

Finally, Dad looked around and teased, "Well, I guess that's it. Let's clean up."

"Daaaaaad!!!" the boys yelled in stereo.

Dad laughed and looked at Mom, "Well, maybe we could find one more for each of them?"

Mom instructed the boys to close their eyes, and Dad slipped out of the room to retrieve the last two gifts. When he returned, Dad and Mom both counted, "One... Two... Three... Open your eyes!"

In front of each boy stood a perfect, gleaming new bike, complete with all the bells and whistles (literally). Cory gasped with delight, jumped on his bicycle, and immediately started riding around – well, as much as Mom would let him ride in the house. He was thrilled beyond words.

Evan, however, had a surprisingly different reaction. He stood up, walked around the bike, quietly examining it, and then stood still, staring at the floor.

"What's wrong, Evan?" Mom asked, confused by his reaction.

Evan stuttered, trying to restrain his emotions, until he couldn't take it anymore. He suddenly burst into tears, sobbing uncontrollably, until he could finally get the words out: "I...(hiccup)... was really...(sniff)... hoping for...(deep breath)... a new car!"

Dad was flabbergasted. Looking at Mom, he asked, "What new car? Was there a different toy he asked for?" Mom shook her head, shrugged her shoulders, and looked to Evan for the answer.

"N-n-no..." he sobbed, "I wanted a new car ... just like the one Dad just got!" Barely finishing his sentence, he burst back into a new wave of tears in melodramatic fashion.

Dad and Mom exchanged looks of disbelief. Just a month earlier, they had purchased a new sedan for Dad to use for his daily commute. And now their seven-year-old is throwing a tantrum because he wanted one, too?

IMPATIENT AND IMPRACTICAL

I am sure you're wondering what in the world this story about the unrealistic expectations of a selfish little kid has to do with you as a single adult. I'm also sure that even if you don't have children yet, you have seen similar displays of "gratitude" from a child you've known at one point or another. They didn't get the right toy in their kid's meal; they didn't get the flavor of lollipop they wanted; they didn't get as big of a cookie as the other kid got. When it comes to getting what they want, kids can be so impatient and so impractical. *Can't you just make my brother give me his candy so I'll have the flavor I want? Can't you just drive back to the store and buy the kind of juice I like?*

Children can have such short fuses emotionally, and the least little disappointment can trigger a full-blown meltdown. Of course, it is tempting for us adults to frown and think, *What a spoiled little brat,* and want to take everything away from them to teach them how to be grateful. But hey, this isn't a book about child psychology, so we won't spend too much time rationalizing Evan's reaction. Let's just tie things together and make sense of how this applies to us.

A CHILDLIKE HEART

One thing I've observed in children is that as great as their tendency is toward sensational displays of disappointment and ingratitude, children are also prone to exaggerated expressions of joy and appreciation! Just think about a three-year-old little girl beaming as she shows her Mommy the five new pennies someone at church gave her. It doesn't even matter to her that her big sister got one dime. In her mind, she got exactly what she wanted, and she couldn't be more pleased!

Our perceptions of the gifts we are given grow and change as we do. Eventually, that little girl will realize that five pennies won't buy her much. At that point, she'll probably start receiving token gifts of higher value. Maybe Grandma slips her a dollar every time she comes to visit (while Grandpa sneaks her two dollars before she leaves). A few more years down the road, this girl becomes a teenager, and her birthday cards will probably start bearing ten- and twenty-dollar bills instead of ones or fives. The gifts change based on what she is able to appreciate and responsibly manage. Looking back, we might ask how five pennies were meaningful or how a dollar made a difference. But the great part is that, in her mind, the gifts were fabulous all along, because each gift showed that someone cared, that someone was taking notice of her. The gifts changed as she changed, and we're no different. The gifts we receive in life are directly proportional to the season we are in and our level of maturity; if we can understand that, then we can fully appreciate each and every gift along the way.

THE PERFECT GIFT AT THE PERFECT TIME

Think for a minute about our sweet little friend, Evan. Was that a true story? Of course not. What seven-year-old is going to turn down a shiny new bicycle because he thought he was going to get a new car? He can't even drive yet! What child is going to reluctantly take the bike and ride it around, all the while moaning, "This isn't the new car I asked Daddy for, but –" (sniff, sniff) "– I'll just keep persevering until he sees fit to give me what I really asked for"? No kid I know would act like that. However, I've known all too many single adults who have acted exactly like that, and I'm not proud to say I have been one of them.

See, Dad knows (and we all know) that for this season of his son's life, the bicycle is the perfect, most appropriate gift he could give him. Giving Evan a real car to drive now would not only be an inappropriate gift and an extraordinary waste of money, but it would also be a dangerous, life-threatening gift for seven-year-old Evan to have. So instead, Dad gives Evan the bike, and real-life Evan would more than likely do exactly what Dad expected: Throw himself onto the bicycle and, with all the melodrama in him, exclaim, "Oh! This is *great*! It's *exactly* what I wanted!"

Evan does not even have a fleeting thought about wanting or needing a car. Of course, as he gets closer and closer to his sixteenth birthday, he will most likely have a car on the brain. Even so, although Evan may start thinking more and more about that car in the coming years, Dad will be sure not to give it to him until it is the appropriate time for him to have it, when

Evan is fully skilled, equipped, and prepared to handle such a gift responsibly and safely.

See, what Evan may not realize and what we often miss is that the bicycle is not a consolation prize while he waits out the next nine years until he's 16. The bicycle is Evan's training ground. Learning to navigate, becoming more aware of his surroundings, yielding to cars when he's riding on the side of the street – All these things will help equip Evan physically and mentally with skills that will be very valuable when he begins operating a vehicle in the years ahead. What Dad is really doing here is trusting Evan with a new level of independence. He's handing him a gift to use to explore his surroundings, to build his muscles, to exercise his physical body and his mental awareness in ways that Evan couldn't do by just walking down to the cul-de-sac. The bicycle is a thrill for Evan! It signals Dad's trust in him, and even if he gets a few scrapes along the way, it is a tool that Dad can use to teach Evan important principles he will carry with him long after he retires his little kid bicycle.

THE GIFT OF SINGLE

We can use Evan's story to understand how fully our Father loves us and cares for us. God knows how old I am and how prepared I am to handle each of the gifts He has lined up for me. Just as Evan's father is not going to hand him the car keys at age seven or even age fourteen, my Father is not going to hand me the gift of Marriage until He knows I am fully equipped and ready for all that it will bring; He knows that doing so prematurely would set me up for devastation and disaster, and He loves me too much to do that. Furthermore,

He's probably not going to hand me the gift of Marriage until I've proven that I'm both appreciative and responsible with the gift He has already given me, the gift of Single.

Even though we like to think we are ready *right now,* how many of us have been like the unrealistic Evan, throwing big-girl temper tantrums in front of our heavenly Father, because we're still "stuck" with this same ol' gift we've been asking Him to take away for all these years now? I know we like to think that we're so mature, but seriously (unless I'm the only one out here on this limb by myself), how many times have we begged God to please just do whatever is necessary to bring our husbands to us, and *soon?!* And then, if you're prone to overanalyzing like I am, you've probably taken it a step further, doing God a favor by defining in your prayers what "*soon*" means: "...by the time I'm 21." When that didn't happen, my prayers changed to, "...Please, God, by the time I'm out of college." When that didn't happen, "...Please, *please,* Lord, don't make me wait past my 25th birthday." Well, I began writing this book shortly after I turned 26, so that obviously didn't happen, either. Rather than continue to pointlessly attach deadlines to my prayers, I finally gave up putting God on my timeline and surrendered my preconceived ideas of when things were supposed to happen.

"But I've been asking for so long!" you might say.

I understand. But maybe you need to be honest with yourself and admit that when it comes to embracing Single and waiting for Marriage, you, too, have treated our Father's gift of Single like Evan treated his bike. Maybe you've pouted like a little kid, bemoaning the fact that your Father didn't love you enough to give you what you really wanted. Maybe you've pedaled around on your shiny, gleaming gift of Single, all the while wiping tears from your eyes and holding back the sobs, not understanding why you couldn't just have that new car right now. Maybe you've even been ashamed to let your other friends know that you've got this awesome bike, because you're afraid they're going to make fun of you and dangle their car keys in your face. Let's be honest. We may be grown adults, but at times, our emotional maturity level hasn't been far off from Evan's in terms of our Father's gift of Single. It's easy for us as adults to understand why a child can't have everything they want right now, but it takes some extra maturity for us to realize that this is the exact same reason *we* can't have everything we want right now.

Most of us, if we let our minds go unrestrained, could probably drive ourselves insane simply from fear and worry: fear of the unknown, fear of "what ifs," fear of being single forever, fear of being alone, fear of God the Father forgetting about the desires of our hearts.

I want to assure you today that our Father is standing before you, and He hears every prayer you've prayed; He's seen every tear you've cried as you've longed for Him to send you your lifelong companion. Sometimes we misconstrue His refusal to give us what we're asking for as indifference toward us. In reality, it is a demonstration of how greatly He loves us! He loves us so much that He isn't simply going to give us what we asked for just to shut us up! If I can use another kid analogy, think of the child throwing a tantrum in the middle of the restaurant, whose parent ends up giving him whatever it is he wants just so he'll stop it already. Most of us understand that even if you want to make a kid happy, you can't give him everything he asks for instantly, because immediately appeasing him in this way builds no character in him. See, God loves us too much to give us our every whim when we ask for it, because He cares not only about making us happy; He also cares about the persons we are becoming, the character He is building in us.

So instead, He is looking at us, eyes filled with patient love toward us, and asking, "What are you doing with the gift I've already given you?" While we're pointing at the car in our future, He's pointing at the shiny new bicycle right in front of us, waiting to see if we will use it to its full advantage and potential.

Single isn't His consolation prize to us. He chose it for us, very deliberately and purposefully, because He has plans for this very special gift He has presented to us. He wants to use this gift of Single as a training ground to equip us with valuable skills, experiences, and knowledge that we can then carry with us for the rest of our lives. He knows that if He gives us the next gift too early, we will be ill-prepared for the coming years, and we will have a much harder time navigating the rest of our lives than if we would just learn some solid principles now. We would do well to embrace this gift and allow our Father to show us and teach us valuable life skills, instead of impatiently ignoring the opportunity in front of us and trying to make the next season happen on our own.

I think you will agree that many people have rushed ahead into Marriage before they were truly ready, and the results were just as disastrous as if Evan had driven a new car around the block that Christmas morning. Perhaps you yourself have even rushed into Marriage and have experienced the difficulties firsthand. If you've been in a relationship that ended disastrously, if you've had a failed marriage, or if you've been close to someone who has, then you know that the danger is real. Not only is the danger real to us, but it is real to others around us, just as if an oncoming car is being driven by a seven-year-old who can't quite see over the dashboard and reach the pedals at the same time. How many of us have been impacted by a marriage that fell apart? How many children's lives have been devastated by their parents' marriage being ripped apart? How many of us know someone who got trapped in a starry-eyed relationship that turned abusive and controlling? While it's easy to identify the mistakes other people have made by rushing into relationships, it's much harder for us to realize that perhaps the reason we aren't married yet is that our Father is still getting us ready so that we can avoid those same kinds of mistakes.

See, what we have often thought was God's lack of love and attentiveness toward us has actually been His loving protection over us. He is constantly shielding us from dangers that we don't see, as long as we will remain under His protection and not remove ourselves in our short-sighted haste.

THE FATHER ONLY GIVES GOOD GIFTS

No matter where you're at today, there is one thing I know for sure about our Father: He is good, and He will only do what is best for us.

Jesus says in Matthew 7:9-11:

> *Which of you, if your son asks for bread, will give him a stone? Or if he asks for a fish, will give him a snake? If you, then, though you are evil, know how to give good gifts to your children, how much more will your Father in heaven give good gifts to those who ask him!*

What Jesus is doing here is showing us the heart of our Father. In case your father here on earth wasn't this way – maybe he was absent, abusive, or just plain oblivious – Jesus wanted to be sure He explained to us what a true father is like. If a child asks for something to eat, a true father isn't going to give the kid a rock and then point and laugh at his disappointment and misery! A father takes care of his children; he takes care of both their basic needs and the desires that he's able to fulfill.

If we let them, these words can really shift our perception of Single. If we trust Jesus' words in this passage, then we know that God does indeed hear our prayers. For those of us who are praying and asking Him for a spouse, we can trust that He only gives us *good* gifts. So often, we are duped into thinking that Single is the snake God gave us when we asked for a fish. It's just not true! If we asked for Marriage and all we have right now is Single, we need to keep in mind that the Father only gives us good gifts, so Single must be intended to be good!

There's a reason He handed us Single and hasn't handed us Marriage yet, and the reason undoubtedly revolves around what is best for us! Ultimately, we have to trust His timing. If we will be patient and seek Him first, He will take care of the rest. Remember Jesus' instruction and promise to us in Matthew 6:33:

> *But seek first his kingdom and his righteousness, and all these things will be given to you as well.*

While you're waiting for the next gift you've asked for, what are you doing with the gift He's already given you? What are you doing for the Kingdom of God?

Remember, unlike most gifts, when our Father does see fit to hand us the gift of Marriage, we will have to trade in the gift of Single forever. We may never get this opportunity again, and we certainly won't get it again in the way it is being presented to us right now.

I encourage you today to join me in adjusting our perspective. Let's jump on our bikes of Single, ride down the sidewalk with the wind billowing in our hair, and don't forget to blow some kisses to our Father as we pass by Him, waving and thanking Him for this fabulous and quite perfect gift we have right now! There's a world of joy and adventure waiting for us in whatever time left that we have in Single. Won't you join me in embracing and enjoying it?

So be careful how you live. Don't live like fools, but like those who are wise. ***Make the most of every opportunity...*** *And give thanks for everything to God the Father in the name of our Lord Jesus Christ.*
Ephesians 5:15-16, 20 (NLT)

Chapter Two

VILLAINS & VICTIMS:
THE ENEMY CALLED SINGLE

let God weigh me in honest scales...
Job 31:6

Our culture has presented us with a brutal, false perception of what Single is supposed to be. Truthfully, they've got it all wrong. How we tend to feel about Single is completely contrary to how God the Father intended it to be for us. Take, for instance, the following scenarios (which you have undoubtedly seen, if not in real life, then numerous times in movies and on television):

> **Scenario 1.** Girl is living life, seemingly okay, but not dating. Girl's friends give her a hard time for not having a date for the upcoming weekend, or maybe for not having dated in months, or maybe even for not having had sex in such a long time (if ever). So the girl who was okay is now keenly aware of her singleness and becomes restless. Girl meets boy. Girl falls for boy. Boy "rescues" girl from the horrible curse of Single that she had been living in for so long.

> **Scenario 2.** Boy and girl meet. Boy and girl date for a while – maybe only a few weeks, maybe a few months, or maybe even a few years. Something goes wrong. Either boy is not ready for commitment, there is some huge misunderstanding, or maybe boy cheats on girl. Boy and girl break up. Girl lives in heartbreak and

heartache until new boy comes along. Repeat entire story.

Repeat again.

And again ...

> **Scenario 3.** Girl is heartbroken from a situation like Scenario 2. Girl hardens her heart toward men, marriage, and relationships, and she attempts to live life focused on her own goals and career. Then one day, her walls are broken down when true romance is found again, thus rescuing her from herself.

The story lines change, but the theme is constant: No one can be happy or complete without romance in her life. We are bombarded with these sorts of scenarios. We see constant portrayals of single people who are miserably enduring life until that special someone comes along. So we attempt to live by following the same mindsets and patterns. We begin to think that Single is God's miserable punishment on us or at least a trial He has handed down to us to endure. We become consumed with our state of Single, and unfortunately, that obsession results in a cycle of broken relationships, broken hearts, and broken people.

THE BAD GUY

In our society, Single is commonly perceived as the bad guy. It seems to be the one thing that almost everyone in our culture is anxious to abandon. Even for those independent souls who don't want to settle down, commit, and get married, they don't typically want to be entirely alone, either. Almost everyone is longing, pining, and even jockeying for relationship – anything to keep from being slotted in that lonely sector of life called Single. Disdained by many, the Single status shapes our opinions of ourselves, defines or restricts our abilities, and limits our dreams. Our awareness of our position can be so great that just the simple act of filling out a form and reaching that dreaded line for "marital status" can bring waves of discouragement as we reluctantly check the box, "Single."

Even in Christian circles, we tend to get trapped, focusing so much on the season *beyond* Single that we never truly learn to enjoy and embrace the season of Single for what it really is, a gift to us from our Creator and Father. Church becomes useful, first and foremost, as a pool of potential soul mates; for some, it becomes so extreme that when they run out of options at one church, they switch churches to find a fresh batch of single, Christian men to scout out. Their social lives at church become a string of one dead-end attempt connected to another, and they don't even recognize or benefit from the life-giving connection a church family really should be for them. Even as Christians, hoping and trying to follow God's will for our lives, we drive ourselves to the brink of insanity, because we can't seem to shake this desperation we feel for companionship.

I'm happy to tell you today, from my own experience, that we don't have to continue to live in this miserable way. God never meant for Single to be a curse; it is truly a gift from Him. It took me a long time to realize that shunning Single was, in essence, shunning the Giver of the gift as well. In this journey, we are going to learn that Single is not the bad guy in our life, and Marriage is not the cure-all for the feelings we've wrestled for so long.

Are you ready to let things get really, well, real? If so, then here we go…

LEVEL WITH YOURSELF

You are not in a holding pattern. That's worth repeating: You are not in a holding pattern. Let's face it: If we are going to live out this season with joy, contentment, and fulfillment, then we have to be willing to examine ourselves first and recognize things that we should be doing differently. So let's jump in, face some facts, and get rid of some of our own melodrama about our relationship with Single. Here are three important facts to get us started:

1. **Life is not passing you by.** That is, life is not passing you by unless you're *letting* it. If life is passing you by, then you must not be moving! And if you aren't moving, it's only because you are choosing to stay still. Unfortunately, that's what many of us do in Single. We don't see things happening for us the way we always thought they would, so we become overwhelmed and paralyzed in inactivity. We see our entire destiny as being "on hold" until that blissful day when we find our soul mates and can run hand-in-hand into the sunset together (ahem, that is, into the destiny God has for us together). It's time, as women of God, to make the decision to stop wallowing, get up, brush ourselves off, and start moving forward in the direction our Creator is calling us.

2. **If you see Single as trial and tribulation, you need a paradigm shift.** You are not enduring the hardest plight of humanity; neither are you a victim or martyr of the human race. You do not have it harder than everyone else in life. None of this is true simply because you check the box, "Single," for marital status. You may think I'm exaggerating here, but think about it: Have you ever thought your married friends were lucky, because at least they had someone to go home to? At least they had someone to keep them warm at night? **It's all too easy for us in Single to allow our desires to turn from pure longings into miserable envy of what everyone around us has that we think we want.** We have to stay grounded in reality and recognize that what everyone else has (as in, marriage and companionship) does not come without effort and a price. Marriage has not been a fix-all for our friends, and it won't be for us, either. Furthermore, by bemoaning Single, we're doing ourselves a great disadvantage, and we're preparing ourselves to be *unprepared* when we enter marriage. Single is intended to be a training ground for us for the rest of our lives; by doing nothing with the gift in our hands now, we are setting ourselves up for setbacks when the time for marriage comes.

3. **You are in charge of your focus.** Your perspective is in *your* hands. If your focus is off-track, you are the only one who can adjust the direction and re-aim your focus. Thankfully, God doesn't leave us to do it all by ourselves when we need help. You can ask Him, even this very

minute, to help you adjust (or completely overhaul) your focus in every area that He sees fit, starting now.

OBSESSED WITH FINDING THE ONE

As I made my way through college at a Christian university, I found that many of my female peers had one focus and one focus only: to become un-single as quickly as possible! Unfortunately, I spent more than my fair share of time as one of them. The ultimate goal in life was to find a husband – not just any husband, by the way, but to find *the one* God had for me. The problem was that none of us really wanted to wait; we refused to consider that God might want us to stay single longer than we wanted. The only right way in our minds was for God to make it happen *right now!* We assumed that since we wanted it right now, God must want to give it to us right now! If He wasn't giving it to us, then we thought we needed to pray harder, maybe even fast and pray, plead and beg; we would do anything we could think of to convince God we were ready.

It went beyond just a God-given need for companionship; at least for me, it really became an unhealthy obsession. Granted, we still maintained our relationships with God during this time; overall, I know our intentions were good, trying to pursue God in the middle of dealing with our desires for companionship. But I also know that for me personally, I couldn't fathom that instead of answering my prayer right now, God might have wanted to give me grace and faith to wait patiently until His time. I only had "faith" that I would round the next corner and run into Prince Charming, or "faith" that the one I had already picked out across campus would open his eyes any day now and finally see that what he'd been wanting all along was standing right in front of him (ahem, *me*). Of course, he'd fall in love with me, and we'd live happily ever after in love and ministry. Besides, if my desire was to marry and *minister together* for God, then why would God hold that back from me, right? It seemed rational that God would want us to get started on that right away!

Several of us girls were in that boat of good intentions together. We didn't know what was wrong with all these guys around us or why they couldn't see us as the dream-come-true that we were waiting to be for them. Nothing in life felt truly fulfilling, and nothing generated lasting contentment, because we were all restless and anxious to move out of Single and into Marriage. Sure, we were pursuing our degrees and career goals, and because we all loved God, we were still involved in ministry and outreach endeavors on-campus. We didn't completely put our spiritual gifts on the shelf. But, speaking for myself, the desire for companionship very much hindered my effectiveness in reaching out to others. It was always at play in my mind; it was something that, whether in the back of my mind or in the forefront, was constantly a very active awareness in whatever I was doing. I was often distracted as I walked through campus, looking for that special someone, wherever he might be.

See, a desire that was not inherently wrong – the desire to be married – had utterly consumed my mind and emotions and had become a very hindering obsession. This obsession had become my primary focus in life in an extremely unbalanced way. I wrestled with it for a long time myself, and long afterward, I realized that this obsession worked in two ways.

One way was pretty obvious, and the other was much more subtle. Maybe you can relate to one or both.

The "Looking for Love in ALL Places" Obsession

The first and more obvious way the obsession worked was the manner I just described: I went through life, looking around every corner and every turn for that special someone. I can recall times when walking through the grocery store, I would literally glance around every turn and down every aisle, just in case I was about to run into *the one*. The only exception was when I had already locked my affections on some special someone, and still, I spent every waking moment either hoping to run into him unexpectedly or being frustrated over unreciprocated interest. It consumed every aspect of my life.

Proverbs 4:23 says, "Above all else, guard your affections. For they influence everything else in your life" (NLT). There was no truer statement about my life at that point. Deciding what to wear in the morning was influenced by whether or not I thought I'd run into any prospects that day. Deciding whether or not to go with friends to this place or that depended on who I thought would or wouldn't be there. The obsession of looking for love was always at play. *Always.*

There is no human emotion that is quite like the desperation, helplessness, and even despair that a single person feels when she decides on her own that she should no longer be single. The outcome can be dangerous and destructive. Needless to say, in those times of my life, I accomplished very little for the sake of the rest of humanity. With my focus only on *my* need to find love and companionship, it is a miracle that I ever focused on academics and other endeavors. Looking back, I see now how miserable it was to be ruled by that obsession, and I wonder how much more productive and successful I could have been if I had learned how to surrender that obsession to God sooner rather than later. The discontentment was captivatingly distracting and tried to divert me from moving forward in my true destiny.

That was the first way the obsession with becoming un-single worked in me. Maybe you can relate to it. But obsessive desires can work in another, sneakier way, too, especially for those of us who have been immersed in our church culture.

The Anti-Desire Obsession

Filled with good intentions, we Christian college girls unwittingly succumbed to this more subtle form of the un-single obsession. Keep in mind that even though our emotions were seemingly in unbridled control of our lives, our hearts really were after God. Most of us had been raised in church, and we really did want to follow God's purposes for our lives. As we began recognizing that "looking for love in all places" was driving us crazy and getting us nowhere, we attempted to correct the problem.

Think back, if you will, to Drivers' Ed class. New drivers are taught that if you ever need to quickly escape a dangerous situation, you should be cautious against over-steering. Over-correction has the potential of causing a more tragic accident than the original predicament would have. The Anti-Desire Obsession is what I call the Christian over-correction to "looking for love in all places."

We began devouring books on abstaining from dating, learning how to wait for our mates, and focusing solely on God and nothing else. Were these materials erroneous in nature? Not necessarily. I learned some good principles in them. But we weren't addressing the core issues. Before long, we were trying so hard *not* to want to be married that our obsession for getting married had not declined at all. Now instead of just being obsessed with marriage, we were obsessed with *not* being obsessed with marriage!

It's as if you tell a person, "Don't think about purple, polka-dotted elephants." What are you thinking about? Of course, you're thinking about purple, polka-dotted elephants! Although my intentions were good in trying to become un-obsessed with getting married, I was still unable to achieve 100% contentment in Single so that I could focus on becoming the woman of God I am called to be.

Truthfully, my ulterior motive was that I was using those books to try to hurry along the process. My goal was not to enjoy Single; it was to do whatever God could possibly want me to do so He would hurry up and let me get married already! I was still too preoccupied with my worrisome state of Single and how to escape it as quickly as possible. I still couldn't find a way to actually enjoy the season of Single.

As if that weren't enough, here is where the over-correction got really convoluted. Not only did I find myself still obsessed with marriage, but I also began subconsciously associating my God-given desires for marriage as bad desires, even sinful ones. I'm not even talking about sexual or lustful desires. I'm talking about the simple desires, the lifelong dream, of falling in love and becoming a wife some day. I began to fear that these desires were ungodly, because I perceived my desires as coming between myself and God. I felt guilty for wanting companionship with a man, because I felt like my desire should be 100% for God. In my mathematical mind, to desire God 100% meant there was no room for other desires, and to desire anyone else meant I must not desire God 100%.

Inwardly, I felt guilty, feeling that natural, God-given desires for marriage were hindering my walk with God. In fact, I really began to wrestle with whether or not marriage was even a God-ordained part of my future; I feared that for God to have all of me, I would have to give up my desire for a mate (We will discuss this in more detail later).

I didn't realize that the ugly enemy of fear was sneaking in, and that enemy was actually the wedge I was feeling between God and myself. **I subconsciously became afraid that God would never give me marriage because He wanted me all for Himself.** This was a dangerous deception to buy into, because if I wasn't careful, that idea could have bred resentment in me toward the God I was so desperately trying to love and please.

I guess you could say I was trying too hard. Way too hard. Thankfully, God is faithful, and His Love is stronger than our ignorance and naivety! Even though I made a lot of misguided efforts to understand His Love and plan for me, He helped me find freedom from that long, unhealthy season of obsession, and He protected me along the way.

The steadfast love of the Lord never ceases; his mercies never come to an end; they are new every morning; great is your faithfulness (Lamentations 3:22-23 ESV).

Thankfully, God's love for me and His never-ending mercies carried me through this very trying time in my journey of Single. His love eventually overcame all of the confusion and misguided notions running around in my head. He led me into a season of contentment and peace, out of which I learned many of the principles I'm able to share with you now.

WHERE ARE YOU TODAY?

I would guess that most of you have experienced one if not both of these forms of obsession in some way or another, especially those of you who have spent some time around church as a single adult. For many of us, the greatest difficulty is just finding a sense of balance, that place in which we find contentment in the journey, even though we have not yet arrived at one of the places we had hoped we would already be.

We need to understand that God did create the desire and need for companionship and intimacy, but we must distinguish between desires from God and idolizing those desires or even allowing them to become flat-out lust. Yes, I have a very real desire for my future husband, but I now refuse to let that desire consume and overwhelm me! If we let the desire grow out of proportion in our lives, we set ourselves up to "fall in love with the idea of being in love." We begin idolizing the notion of being in love – we love the idea of the romance. By doing so, we set ourselves up for failure in one of two ways:

1. We want companionship so badly that at some point we will compromise our standards, morality, and long-term desires from God simply to seize an immediate opportunity; or

2. We romanticize the notion of being with someone so much that, even if God brought Mr. Right to us, we have idolized an ideal for so long that not even Mr. Right can live up to our expectations of what he should be. Thus, we are ill-prepared to function in the healthy relationship we always dreamed of sharing with him.

So what is the solution? How do we find balance? A few foundational decisions can help us resist obsession and live a balanced life:

Decision 1: Choose to trust your Father.

My grandmother reminded me many times throughout my life, especially in seasons of angst or worry, of her very favorite verse in the Bible. So now I offer it to you:

> *And we know that in all things God works for the good of those who love him, who have been called according to his purpose* (Romans 8:28).

When nothing makes sense emotionally or mentally, you can make a conscious choice to trust God anyway. Trust that He holds the best for you. Trust that He is working for your good, because you love Him and are called according to His purpose. Trust that He isn't setting you up for disappointment in life. Trust that He wants you to live a happy, fulfilled life way more than you even want it.

They say that you never really understand a parent's love for a child until you become a parent. Let's try to imagine it anyway, because that's how God loves us. **Our journey to contentment and trust is linked in a huge way to our understanding of the Father's love for us, His daughters.**

A loving father finds joy and delight in making his children's dreams come true. We have to believe that God finds joy and delight in making *our* dreams come true. So if we're still waiting, He must have a reason for the waiting that's ultimately for our good.

Decision 2: Learn to like yourself.

Some of you may wonder what I could possibly mean and how I could possibly expect you to do that. If you can't look in the mirror and be okay with what you see, if you can't enjoy your own company at times, whether you are in a crowd or all by yourself, you will never be free from the obsession of looking for another person. Instead, you will spend your life looking for someone to make you feel likeable and validated.

The truth is that you have to be satisfied to a large extent with just you and God, regardless of whether anyone else is there. It doesn't mean you don't need people. God created us to need friendships and relationships. But if your need for people is constant and never interrupted by welcome moments of solitude, you may need to examine honestly your overall state of contentment with who you are. Once you can enjoy times alone and can sincerely enjoy platonic friendships (without looking for some ulterior development in the relationship), you will position yourself for a truly healthy relationship with your future spouse, regardless of whether he comes sooner or later.

Maybe you are already painfully aware of how much you dislike yourself. Maybe you find it unfathomable that anyone, including God, could love or even like you, because you yourself cannot escape all of your shortcomings and flaws. If you'll stay with me on this journey, I will give you some keys to help you discover the real Truth about how valuable and wanted you are in the eyes of your Father God. We will discuss some principles that will help you if you are one of the many, many women who have never been able to like yourself.

For now, I urge you to hold on to the fact that you were specifically created by a Father who loves you more than you could ever ask Him to! You don't have to beg for His love or attention. You don't have to worry about your love for Him going unreciprocated, because He loved you first. You don't have to worry about Him leaving you standing there alone, wondering what you did to make Him walk away. He chose *you*. And He has you on this journey right now because of how greatly He loves you.

Decision 3: Look beyond yourself.

If you can take your focus off of you and start looking for ways to reach out and help somebody else - whether it is by giving them a ride to the store, lending a shoulder to cry on, or even by going on a foreign missions trip - you will begin to liberate yourself from the selfishness that oftentimes feeds the worries and obsessions we single people are prone to having. You will find tremendous release and fulfillment when you make a decision to help somebody else. **Few things are as powerful as the statement you make spiritually when you make an intentional effort to take your love for God and direct it to someone else.**

The person who sees herself as a victim will forever be handicapped from helping others in a meaningful way. Our greatest fulfillment comes not simply from a lifelong companion but from using our lives to help our brothers and sisters in the world around us, in whatever means God has given us to do so. So if you feel yourself sinking into a pity party about being single, ask yourself what ability or gift God has given you to help someone else today. There's no better way to crash a pity party than by doing something selfless for someone else! Maybe you need to make a phone call to encourage a friend. Maybe you need to take some unused clothing to a nearby charity. Maybe you need to tell a young teenage girl you know just how much she's worth in the eyes of God. Proverbs 11:25 says:

> *A generous person will prosper;* **whoever refreshes others will be refreshed.**

Whoever you are, whatever your strengths and weaknesses, God has given you the ability to help – to refresh – someone around you. And there's no better way to get your mind off of yourself than to reach out and help someone else!

These three decisions will help us resist obsession with our state of Single. However, the nature of obsession is that we often become tangled in it and don't know how to get out. If that's you, I encourage you to pause right now and very honestly ask God for His help in becoming free from the cords of obsession. His Love can break any web, no matter how entangled you may have become.

If you need help with the words to say, here is just an idea of how you might want to pray:

> *Father, I believe that You love me more than I can imagine. I'm offering myself, Your daughter, to You. I ask You to lead me in this journey. Help me to understand Your love for me. Please free me from the obsessive discontentment that I've had about being single. Open my eyes to see and trust that You hold what's best for me, and please grant me the patience and contentment to wait for Your plan to be fulfilled in my life. My life and my future are in Your hands. Thank You for loving me.*
>
> *In Jesus' Name, Amen.*

Chapter Three
WHAT ARE YOU WORTH?

Cinderella was always her favorite princess. It wasn't only because she had blue eyes and blonde hair like her, and it wasn't only because Cinderella is a lot of little girls' favorite. Maddie could relate to Cinderella's story, and it gave her hope. Orphaned by a tragic car accident when Maddie was only 2 years old and having no extended family to take her in, her entire life had been spent bouncing through "the system."

Now a teenager, she had spent years moving from foster home to foster home, and her dreams of ever knowing the security of having a mother and father were slipping further and further away. She finally gave up believing for the love of a father and began hoping for Prince Charming. If the right one – or *any* one – could come rescue her from this life of temporary acceptance, this life of being accused of things she never did, this life of having her innocence stripped away by men who only knew how to abuse her... this life of not being able to remember the only two people who ever truly loved her, the ones who gave her the limited identity she had... If she could only be rescued and accepted by her very own prince, then she could close the door to this horrible nightmare of a childhood and live happily ever after.

Maddie's worldview had been skewed and distorted by her life experiences. Nothing in life had ever been fair. She clung desperately to the hope that someone would come along, save her, and introduce her to a new reality, one in which she actually enjoyed living. The problem with her dream was that her desperation to escape her current circumstances left her with virtually no judge of character. She couldn't distinguish between a predator and Prince Charming. So she gave her heart over and over to men who only wanted to use her, abuse her, then leave her to pick up the pieces. Maddie was broken. She was confused. And she was very, very alone.

Maddie represents many girls and young women I have known throughout my life and ministry so far. We've all known her. Maybe you have been her.

We've all known the starry-eyed girl who saw only the good in that really sketchy guy. For those of us watching from the outside, the warning signs were not even just red flags; they were huge, flashing lights with sirens screaming at her to stay as far away as possible. But she couldn't see or hear the warnings. We've all seen her run blindly into the relationship, destined to be heartbroken and devastated when he turns out to treat her exactly as we knew he would. Maybe he left her pregnant and alone. Maybe he left her abused. Maybe he left her abandoned or betrayed or cheated. She almost certainly was left feeling much, much further from God than when she started.

What causes a girl to run headlong into an unhealthy relationship? What makes an otherwise intelligent young lady give her heart and maybe even her everything to an undeserving person? I can tell you what *doesn't* cause her to do that: Love. True Love is not entirely blind. While it may see through a lot of faults (thank God, right?), True Love does not make excuses for lack of integrity, for immorality, or for weak character.

So if it's not Love that causes the young girl to fall headlong into the wrong relationship, then what is it?

It's her perception of her own *value*. She doesn't recognize her worth.

PERCEIVED VALUE

Our perception of value largely influences our actions and decisions. What do I mean by that? Think about this. If you were going through a drive-thru, reached out to pay the cashier, and accidentally dropped a penny, would you open the car door and get it? What if it had rolled under the car out of reach? To what lengths would you go to get that penny? Most of us would probably just pull out another penny, or perhaps the cashier would tell us not to worry about it, and we would drive off. We'd probably never think about that penny again. But if you were in a drive-thru paying the cashier, and your engagement ring fell off and rolled under the car, to what lengths would you go to get it? Would you even for a moment consider driving off without it? How we perceive something's value determines how we treat it.

Here's another example. If someone handed you an envelope with a piece of paper in it, you probably wouldn't rush home to lock it up in a safe. You probably wouldn't rush to the bank to lock in their vault ... unless it was a very valuable savings bond, or perhaps a historical document signed by one of America's founding fathers, or maybe a personal check from a famous billionaire who wrote out a generous donation directly to you. In those cases, even something as simple as a signature can cause an ordinary piece of paper to go from being trash to being an item of extreme value, and you would go to great lengths to protect it from theft or loss, wouldn't you? In reality, it's still "just" a piece of paper, but its value has changed significantly.

Too many of us are running around thinking we're just a random piece of paper – just circumstantial flesh and bones. We let whoever comes by mess with us, crumple us up, or maybe make a paper airplane out of us, until they get tired of us and toss us to the side.

What we fail to realize is that, more significant than the artist's signature on a famous painting or the signature on that billionaire's check, **we are marked by the signature of God, the Creator of the entire universe.** You may look at yourself on the outside and see a mere mortal human, but His unique plans are etched into you, into your personality, your gifts, your skills, and even your physical body.

We have to understand that our imperfections do not have any effect on our value. We often think that we are less valuable to God or even to our future mates because of the mistakes we've made, because of the problems we have, or even because of the lack of talent or abilities we have to offer. We must change our thinking. Did you know it is actually possible to be aware of your imperfections without despising or loathing yourself?

Let me be real. I've struggled much of my life with carrying too much weight, whether it was just being a tad overweight throughout high school or being a lot overweight at times already in adulthood. However, while I have been keenly aware of my imperfections and the need and benefits for changing these things, I have rarely struggled with self-image. I mean, sure there are those days when I'm just fed up about it and could kick myself for not sticking to that diet I started last year. There are definitely those days I don't even step on the scale, because let's be honest; I just don't want to know. But most days, even if I've failed miserably at my efforts to improve myself, I can still look in the mirror and be okay with what I see, even though I'm looking directly at my own flaws and results of my own poor choices. How is that so? **I learned early on that my value isn't tied to my imperfections, and neither is yours.** Our value is in *who* we are, not in the imperfections we see in ourselves. Let me give you one more example to drive this home.

Think about a $100 bill. Now, I know, there's just something about holding a crisp, unused bill in your hand that makes some people's pulse race a little faster. But truthfully, does the crisp, perfect $100 bill have any greater value than the crumpled up, imperfect $100 bill? Nope. They are both worth exactly the same. If you go to the mall and offer the crisp bill to the cashier at your favorite store, you are not going to get any special favors or any more merchandise by paying with that bill than if you pay with the imperfect bill. Why? Because the value isn't determined by the bill's current condition; the value isn't even determined by whose hands the bill has passed through. The value was determined in the beginning when the bill was created. Before that bill of currency was released to start circulating and serving its purpose in life, it was marked with a value that could never be revoked by anyone other than the entity that created it.

Your value isn't determined by your current condition, either; your value isn't even determined by who has used you. Your value was determined in the beginning by your Creator, and no one can ever revoke your value to Him.

Understanding your value is what enables you to be confident in who you are and empowers you to protect yourself from predators and abusers, even though your past may not be picture-perfect. When you understand how valuable you are to your Creator, you begin to see that *His* opinion of you is the only one worth living for.

SELF-PERCEPTION

So let me ask you: How do you see yourself? So many of us have been burned, scarred, and sometimes left for dead as victims of very wrong relationships.

Your best defense against wrong relationships is to know your worth.

For some of you, that statement may as well be written in a foreign language, because up until now, you have had no concept of how worthy you are of the *right* relationship.

For others of you, you may have been clued in on the fact that you have value, but perhaps you have ignored your value for the sake of the moment, or maybe circumstances have caused you to forget your value.

Most of us dreamed dreams when we were younger about the man who would sweep us off our feet and carry us away to be married. Some of us even made detailed lists of qualities and characteristics we look for in our future spouse. However, many if not all of us have, at some point or another, left those dreams and desires behind in order to enter into a "less-than" relationship. We wanted to escape Single sooner rather than later, so instead of waiting for Mr. Right, we settled for Mr. Right-Now. It is quite a dangerous thing to compromise your own value and worth simply for the sake of the moment. In fact, remember the breakup I shared with you in the Introduction? This is exactly how that relationship got started. Let me explain.

This is the only real dating relationship I have had so far in my life, and it began, basically, because I decided I had waited long enough. Now at the time, there seemed to be much more complicated factors than just that. But the bottom line was this: I was 23 years old, had never "officially" dated anyone before, had never even kissed a boy, and I was now becoming afraid that I was going to get too old before I got married. Having always dreamed of getting married young and then having four children, I decided God might need some help moving things along. So in spite of all my dreams for my future husband and marriage, when this guy showed a romantic interest in me, I didn't want to push the opportunity away and keep waiting for who-knows-how-long. He was right there in front of me right then, he was a Christian who seemed to be actively seeking God's will for his life, and he actually was attracted to *me*; at the time, that seemed like a good enough combination for me. I knew that on many levels he did not match the dreams God had put in my heart, but I compromised my value for the moment. I was tired of waiting.

See, here is the thing: The real issue was not that I was getting too old or too lonely. The real issue was not even that he was a bad guy. The real issue was that I forgot how much I am worth. I knew, somewhere inside of me, from the moment he and I started dating, that something was not right. My parents tried to caution me. My dear, trusted pastors tried to warn me that the relationship wasn't God's best for us. My closest friendship suffered, because I'm sure even she could see that things weren't right. In spite of all of these warning signs, I was too caught up in my own desires and curiosity; I just had to see if this thing could work. Just a few weeks into the relationship, we were looking at potential wedding dates and talking about long-term plans. It was exciting to dream and plan together! Deep down, I still had this nagging feeling, though; I knew he was not the one God had prepared me for, and I was not the one God had for him. Yet my own fears and insecurities (and stubbornness and maybe even rebellion) led me to push all of that knowledge aside to do what I *wanted*, to make myself "happy."

It was God's absolute mercy and grace (and I would dare say the prayers of a fervently praying mother and grandmother) that kept the two of us from entering into a sexual relationship while we were dating, and it was His mercy and grace that brought our relationship to an end before any of our marriage plans began to materialize. I've thanked my Father God countless times over for sparing me the additional sin and baggage that could have resulted from that relationship. I still had my fair share of repenting to do, because it was my own stubbornness that led me into the heartbreak that followed, which you read about earlier. That relationship ended as suddenly as it started, but it left me with broken pieces that were not broken before the relationship began, including fragmented friendships that took much longer to repair than it did to break them. It left me with some hard lessons learned, lessons I wish I would have just learned by listening to the wisdom and counsel of those around me in the first place.

See, I had forgotten that God values me as greatly as He does. I forgot that I was worth more than just, *Well, we can make it work.* I remember actually thinking at times during that relationship, *Is this what I've waited my whole life for?* I tried to push the inner disappointment to the side, but I couldn't make it go away. After 23 years of saving myself and waiting for *the one*, I couldn't help but feel a little let down at how things were going. Again, I am not insulting the guy himself; remember, I was not God's best for him, either. I am simply describing the relationship. It was only after it was over that I realized **the problem was not as much him *or* me as it was him-*and*-me.** Our attempt to be together was not God's best for either of us, and by trying to walk together when we weren't called to do so, we were disrupting God's plan for both of our lives. God had to remind me that I am worth waiting for His best for me, even if it takes longer than I want.

How often have you known a couple, either dating or married, and – not judging merely by appearances – thought they were oddly and unequally paired? He may be such a sensitive, caring man, yet his wife is harsh, manipulative, and self-centered. Or what about the beautiful, intelligent teenage girl with her boyfriend: the lazy, unmotivated "slacker"? How about a devoted, loving mother and her abusive, alcoholic husband? Somewhere, somehow, we are forgetting what we're worth. We see something in front of us, and out of fear that we are not good enough to ever get this chance again, we jump and seize "less than God's best" for us. **We can avoid a lifetime of consequences or hardship by realizing the value each one of us holds in our Father God's eyes.**

DREAMING OF GOD'S BEST

We've got to go back and remember who our Creator is – our Father. We have to remember the dreams we dared to dream in innocence, or for some of us, we have to dare to start dreaming them for the first time: the knight in shining armor, the princess awaiting her prince, the happily ever after.

But life is not a fairy tale, you may argue. I agree! Our dreams need to be grounded in reality. However, the status quo we have been handed for love and marriage is a far cry from what our Father planned for His sons and daughters to have. There is so much beyond what we have been presented by our society. Ladies, you are worth waiting for, and he is worth your wait! If you will make a commitment to settle for **nothing less than God's best**, you will be so richly rewarded. I have no doubt in my mind that when God's best for me does come to fulfillment, my marriage will be light years ahead of where so many in our generation have started out in marriage, not because I am some great human being, but because I trust my Father's plan for me. If nothing else, I will have the solid peace of *knowing* that this man is the man I have waited for, the man I refused others for, the man I held out for. I promise you, on the day I get married, I will not simply be going through a ceremony. I will be looking into the eyes of the man I have prayed for all my life, the man God spared me for in spite of my own failures, and the man that, deep in the innermost chambers of my heart, I have loved all my life. Does that sound too romantic, too good to be true? I assure you, it is not. I know my value. I challenge you to recognize yours and dare to dream just as elaborately. Dare to put your faith out there to your Creator. Let Him know that you will hold yourself in high esteem if He will carry you by His Grace! Ask Him for His help in waiting for Him to lead you to your Best. Most importantly, let Him reveal to you the value you hold in His heart.

...to bestow on them a crown of beauty instead of ashes,
the oil of joy instead of mourning,
and a garment of praise instead of a spirit of despair.
Isaiah 61:3

Chapter Four

FINDING YOURSELF
IN THE HEART OF THE FATHER

I will be a Father to you,
and you will be my sons and daughters,
says the Lord Almighty.
2 Corinthians 6:18

To truly understand our value, we have to start seeing ourselves through the eyes of our Father. To see through His eyes, we have to understand His heart.

Maybe you're like Maddie, and it's hard to understand the heart of a true father, because you've never experienced one in your own life. Maybe your father was absent. Maybe he was physically present in the home but mentally disengaged, distracted by work or hobbies or busyness. Maybe he was abusive. Maybe he was an alcoholic. Maybe he had good intentions but didn't know how to affirm you as his daughter. Maybe he tried to buy your love with gifts and nice things but never knew how to open his heart and love you the way you craved being loved.

If you didn't grow up in a home with a loving father, then I can understand how this paradigm shift is hard for you to relate to, but I assure you, it's not impossible. For others of you, you know what it's like to have a dad who always looks out for you, always loves you, and always takes an interest in the things that interest you. There truly is a very special bond between dads and their daughters. I can't thank God enough for my dad. I believe the father-daughter relationship was intended by God to be a model of what He wants our relationship with Him to look like. But if you've not known the love of a true father, of having a real "dad" in your life, don't give up on knowing this kind of love and acceptance! There is an awesome promise God has given to all of us:

> *Father to the fatherless, defender of widows – this is God, whose dwelling is holy. God places the lonely in families...* (Psalm 68:5 – 6 NLT).

No matter what your experiences have been, I want to show you two very important things about the heart of a true father.

1. **A father loves all of his children wholly and equally.** There may have been times growing up when I did something wrong and my sister did something right, or vice versa, but never – not once – did I feel like my dad loved one of us more or less than the other. One thing was sure: He loved both of us with all of his heart, and to this day, he'll go to any length necessary to help one of his girls if he thinks we need him. Whether it's fixing something on our car or flying across the country to help in crisis, we know he'll be there if we ask him.

   We see this same heart in our Father God (only greater, because of course, He is not confined to imperfections as our earthly fathers are). We see that His love is offered to all, and in Acts 10:34, Peter emphasizes, "I see very clearly that God shows no favoritism" (NLT). God loves all of us, His daughters, with all of His heart, completely and equally.

2. A father's love does not change based on his children's actions. Yes, a father will be proud when his kid does something great. Yes, a father will be disappointed when his kid intentionally disobeys or rebels against him. Yes, a father will correct and discipline his child (which is actually an act of love in and of itself, according to Proverbs 3:12: "because the Lord disciplines those he loves, as a father the son he delights in." Also see Proverbs 13:24 and 23:13 – 14). The mistake we make is in thinking that our actions could possibly change how much our Father loves us. **A father may be disappointed in his child's actions, but a true father is never disappointed *in his child*.**

We see this in the example of the Father's love that Jesus showed us when He spoke of the Prodigal Son (Luke 15:11 – 32). The father in this story had been deeply wronged by his son's actions. I mean, seriously. The son had gone beyond just being a selfish brat. He demanded his inheritance while his father was still living, then he left home and went off and squandered it all on senseless partying and temporary thrills. Not a smart guy, huh? Nevertheless, the father was more eager for his son's return than the son even was. The son committed many sins that could have caused the father great embarrassment, humiliation to the family name, and grave disappointment. The father, however, was more interested in his son's wellbeing than in the severity of his son's actions against himself and the family. When the son, humbled and undoubtedly humiliated by his streak of bad decisions, decided to return home, the father was watching and waiting for him; he literally ran out to meet his son with open arms to welcome him back home where he belonged (v. 20).

You must know – and if you don't know it yet, then choose to begin to believe it – that your Father God loves you every bit as much as He loves anyone else, and nothing you can do can ever shake His love for you! His priority is always your wellbeing; He is always looking out for your best interest, no matter how much shame and disgrace you think you may have caused Him by your own actions or attitudes toward Him.

His Word promises that nothing can ever separate us from His love (Romans 8:38 – 39). How awesome it is to find a Love that unconditional! There's no pressure to perform, no pressure to please. All of our actions can now flow out of our love for our Father, because we can rest securely in His Love for us.

FINDING YOURSELF IN THE PAGES OF GOD'S STORY

To help you see yourself through God your Father's eyes, I want to invite you on a little journey of discovery here. Maybe you identify with the Prodigal Son, and you're already beginning to see the greatness of the Father's Love for you. To open our eyes even more to the Father's heart toward us, I want to show you examples of women in the Bible, all of whom God loved fiercely. As we meet each one, I want you to try to find yourself in these women's stories. You may relate to one of them more than others, or you may relate to pieces of the stories from several of them. Just keep in mind, as you place yourself in their shoes, that every one of them was marked by the Love of God on her life.

1. **Mary, the mother of Jesus.** A young virgin, pledged to be married, Mary was highly favored by the Lord (Luke 1:26 – 28). You might relate to Mary if you've strived to live a life of purity, if you've sought to do things God's way, if you've walked reverently before God, seeking His plan for your life.

   It is very common today for people to respect and even worship Mary; however, society does little to uphold her lifestyle as an example for young girls to live by in today's sex-saturated culture. Imagine if daughters today were taught that Mary was the role model to follow! Instead of filling their minds with almost-nude celebrities parading themselves vulgarly across a stage while crowds go wild, imagine if our young girls were shown the beauty and strength of purity, the power of submitting wholly to God's plan for our lives.

   Nonetheless, there are more of you Marys out there than you think. You may feel like you're the only virgin left – the only one still holding out for marriage – but I assure you, you aren't the only one. God's call to purity is still strong for many. There are blessings in store for you in return for your patience, and your purity brings a power that you would do well not to underestimate.

   Mary didn't have it all easy, however. Today, we speculate that perhaps in the strict, legalistic culture she lived in, she may have been subjected to intense scrutiny, gossip, and judgment when the townspeople found out this young teenage girl was pregnant before she and Joseph were married. We don't know the personal struggles that Mary may have been subjected to, even as she carried out the will of God. We do know that later, after she had birthed Jesus, she and her husband had to take Him and flee to another country because of the ones seeking to kill Him. I can't even imagine the horror she had to face as a mother, knowing that the king of her country had sent trained forces to find and kill her son.

Maybe there are pieces of Mary's story you have lived out. Maybe you've been the one everyone was pointing at and talking about, either because you chose purity or because your sin gave you away. Maybe you were the teenage mom, feeling the stares of people as you walked by with no wedding ring on. Maybe you've even felt threatened and endangered by someone seeking to harm you or your family.

Above all, it is important to recognize that Mary was loved and favored by God. Not only that, but she was *trusted* by God. He chose her to do something no one else was given the opportunity to do – to bear from her own body God Himself in the flesh. God loved and trusted Mary. And He loves and trusts you, too.

2. **Esther, Queen of Persia.** Esther has always been one of my favorites. Her story is quite possibly the closest thing to a real-life fairy tale that we see in the Bible. She basically won a beauty pageant, in which the top prize

was becoming the King's wife (as in, the Queen). I mean, really... She didn't need Prince Charming; she just married the king himself!

Esther is an intriguing woman. When we are first introduced to her, we meet an innocent Jewish orphan, raised by her cousin, who taught her God's ways (Esther 2:5 – 7). Somehow, whatever circumstances led to her having neither a father nor mother were not able to harden her toward God. It's clear she possessed an inner beauty, but Esther was also physically beautiful, something some of us long for while others consider a curse.

As her story progresses, we find that she is indeed chosen out of all the young ladies in the land to marry the king. Then, during what is supposed to be the Happily Ever After of the fairy tale, we find Esther fighting not only for her own life, but for the lives of all of her people in Persia (Esther 3). A young woman who seems to have it all is now fighting for survival. And she isn't fighting a typical battle. With her trusted cousin's counsel in her ear, she goes up against both the enemy and the established protocol in the palace: She lays her life on the line to be a voice for her people (Esther 4 – 5, 7).

By the end of the story, we realize that Esther was more than just a pretty face. She had a fight in her that her enemy greatly underestimated. Her courage overcame her fears. Her love for her people overcame her love for herself. She took a giant leap of faith in order to speak up for the people instead of remaining silent to protect her own position in the lush palace.

Maybe you can relate to Esther. Maybe you were always known as the "pretty girl," but you knew deep inside you had a greater purpose than just your looks. Or maybe you've overcome some really difficult circumstances early in life, like losing one or both of your parents. Maybe you've found yourself in places of honor and celebration, having no idea how you got there, or maybe you've found yourself in a position to help people in ways you never expected. Maybe you've had to dig deep for courage to face some really impossible situations, and maybe, even to your own surprise, God has met your faith with His miraculous power.

The point is that Esther was God's daughter. She was protected by Him, from the time she was orphaned all the way to laying her life on the line for the sake of God's people. In an all-or-nothing situation, she went all-in, and God was all-in with her. She was chosen, loved, and trusted by Him. And so are you.

3. **Mary Magdalene.** So maybe you don't see yourself in the first Mary or in Esther. Maybe you're reading those descriptions thinking, *If only!* Maybe Mary and Esther are the ones you always wished you could have been, or maybe they're the ones you always resented, because they seemed too perfect to be true. Maybe you think you've messed up too much to ever be in the same

category as these women of God. If so, I have good news for you, because here's where our journey takes a very special twist.

If you think you've sinned too greatly or you feel far too tainted for the Father to love you, I dare you to compare yourself to the women we see who met Jesus along the way.

Let's start with Mary Magdalene. At some point or another, Mary was demon-possessed. Yep, that's right. Luke 8:2 testifies that Mary was one of several women whom Jesus had cured from demon possession. Once she found deliverance, she stayed close to her Deliverer. In fact, at the scene at the Cross, we find this Mary, right next to Mary the mother of Jesus (Matthew 27:56). Look at that. The formerly demon-possessed lady is standing with the former-virgin-chosen-by-God. They are both standing in the same proximity to the Savior, because He loved them both, wholly and completely. He hung there, dying for both of them. God's Grace had kept one in purity and had restored the other from powers too great for her. They both knew His Love powerfully and in equal measure. Mary Magdalene even got to go, again, side-by-side with Mary the mother of Jesus, to the tomb after Jesus was laid to rest. She was *there* when the angel appeared and told them Jesus had risen (Matthew 28:1 – 7). I love that God granted both of these women equal opportunity in the entire experience of Jesus' death, burial, and resurrection. Two women who started their journey at polar opposite ends of the spectrum ended up walking together, equally close to God the Savior. How awesome is that?

Maybe you need deliverance from something that seems out of your control. Maybe you feel like you're on the brink of insanity. Maybe you're trapped by an addiction that started as something you thought you could manage but now controls you. Maybe you've struggled with mental oppression, inner conflict, and turmoil that are too great for you to control. You may have even made comments like, "I'm still fighting my demons." Regardless of the severity of your struggles, I want you to know that Mary Magdalene's Deliverer is still present today. His Name is Jesus, and He wants to deliver you, too; He's ready to free you from bondage and torment and to restore you to a place of closeness with God. His Love for you is greater than the things trying to control you. You can choose to take the power away from those things and give complete control of your life to Him. Remember, He looks at you with the Love of the Father:

> *You, dear children, are from God and have overcome them, because the one who is in you is greater than the one who is in the world* (1 John 4:4).

Mary Magdalene encountered Jesus, and she was never the same. That day was the first day of the rest of her life. It was the turning point. She never had to look back, because the Love she had received was greater than the control or temptations or powers that had once influenced her so greatly. All of those things were powerless in the face of Love. Today, I pray that the Father's Love for you overcomes all of the things you feel are too strong for you. Release them to Him and run into the arms of your Deliverer. Today begins the rest of your life.

4. **Other women who encountered Jesus.** Mary isn't the only "rogue" woman we see whose life is changed by meeting Jesus.

The woman caught in sexual sin. In John 8, we see religious leaders so pious and arrogant that they actually drag a woman to the middle of the group where Jesus is teaching, and they force her to stand there while they broadcast her sin to everyone (John 8:2 – 6). I suppose they are proud of themselves, either for having trapped the woman or for thinking they are about to trap Jesus. They announce that she has been caught in adultery, and they demand Jesus to respond to the part of the religious law that requires her to be put to death.

Can you imagine? The penalty for sexual sin was death. Imagine the shame, fear, and despair she must be feeling, standing there – maybe not even fully clothed, considering the circumstances – surrounded by a group of judgmental men ready to execute her for her sin. Meanwhile, there's no mention of the man she was caught with – Where is he? How did he get away, but she didn't? The situation doesn't feel fair at all; however, the religious law says that Jesus should let them kill her.

But Love changes everything. Jesus doesn't tell them to disobey their religious laws. He just says, "Let any one of you who is without sin be the first to throw a stone at her" (v. 7). With one statement, He bypasses their demands, exposes their hypocrisy, and cuts straight to the heart of the issue. He Himself is the only one present who meets the qualifications of being without sin (1 Peter 2:22), yet He doesn't pick up a stone to throw. He simply extends the challenge to her accusers. I only wish we could see the expressions on their faces when they realize their trap has backfired. The outcome is worth reading word for word:

> *At this, those who heard began to go away one at a time, the older ones first, until only Jesus was left, with the woman still standing there. Jesus straightened up and asked her, "Woman, where are they? Has no one condemned you?"*
>
> *"No one, sir," she said.*
>
> *"Then neither do I condemn you," Jesus declared. "Go now and leave your life of sin"* (John 8:9 – 11).

This woman knew Love that day unlike any man could have ever offered her in bed; she met Love face-to-face and found out that, unlike anything she could have ever known, Love loved her for who she was, not for what she could do for Him. In the wake of the most terrifying and humiliating consequences of sin that she could have ever imagined, Love loved her. There was no waiting period, no proving period, no cleansing period before

Love would accept her. She was caught in sin, came to the brink of judgment, and instead met Love in-person. Just that fast.

The woman with five previous marriages. Another woman meets the same unexpected Love and Grace when she runs into Jesus while fetching water at her local well (John 4). She is of the wrong ancestry, the wrong ethnicity, and the wrong gender for Jesus to be interacting with her socially. Yet Jesus knows she has a need that she will keep covered up forever if He doesn't confront it. She has built walls up around her heart over the years; we can tell, because when Jesus initiates conversation with her, she first tries to shut Him down:

> *You are a Jew and I am a Samaritan woman. How can you ask me for a drink?* (v. 9).

Jesus persists, because He knows there are deeper issues than her demographic statistics. Even after Jesus makes the conversation *real* – He reads her mail, so to speak, letting her know He knows that she has been married five times and is now with a man who isn't her husband – she still tries to play the religious card to dodge the real issues (v. 20). But Jesus' Love pierces through all of her emotional and religious walls; He simply tears them down, and the story ends with her running back to town to gather the townspeople to come meet this man, the Messiah. In one encounter, she goes from a guarded woman living under stereotypes and previous failures to being the woman who brings many of her own people to Jesus (vs. 28 – 30):

> *And many of the Samaritans of that city believed in Him because of the word of the woman who testified, "He told me all that I ever did"* (v. 39, NKJV).

Maybe you can find yourself in this woman's story. She had been around the block a few times. She'd had five failed marriages and had apparently accepted the stereotypes of her culture against her. But Jesus picked her to be a recipient of God's Love that day, which came through some blatant, heart-searching Truth. As a result, she became the one who led others to Christ!

I don't know how many failed relationships are in your past; I don't know how many walls you've built up around yourself or how many stereotypes have left you feeling trapped and limited in your potential, but I can tell you this: A woman who has known failure and bondage but who comes to know Freedom – Christ Himself – is an unstoppable force in the Kingdom of heaven! A beloved daughter of God, you are not too tainted, too used, or too far-gone for God to completely set free, restore, and fulfill His plans and promises for your life! You can make a difference in other people's lives, simply because you've encountered the Love of the Father!

5. **Eve.** If anyone had reason to feel God's condemnation, it was Eve. I mean, seriously, she gets a really bad rap, doesn't she? How many of us have been blamed for opening the door to sin for the entire human race? If only she hadn't eaten the forbidden fruit, maybe none of

us would be dealing with any of the problems we face today!

Maybe you feel like your own poor choices have set in motion a string of repercussions that have affected those you love most: your parents, your siblings, your children, your friends. Maybe you are living with regrets of how you have hurt those around you by your own bad decisions. Maybe it was an unhealthy relationship you stayed in that caused someone around you pain and suffering. Maybe it was an abusive man that you kept close even though you knew the relationship was toxic. Whatever it was, I have to say: If anyone was ever entitled to feel guilty for her bad choices hurting others, it was Eve.

Not only did Eve lose the trust of her husband, being blamed by him in front of God, and lose her perfect home because of their sin, Adam and Eve's sin paved the way for all of us to be born into sin. But it did something else, too. It paved the way for God to redeem us. Yes, we see God hand down consequences to Adam and Eve for their disobedience (Genesis 3:16 – 19). But He reserved the curse of ultimate defeat for the serpent, the enemy himself. He judged the serpent for deceiving the woman, and to the lying devil himself, God spoke these words of judgment:

> *And I will put enmity between you and the woman, and between your offspring and hers; he will crush your head, and you will strike his heel* (Genesis 3:15).

65

Yes, Eve had consequences to bear for her actions, as did Adam for his. But God put the real judgment on the deceptive snake behind the whole scheme. Ultimately, God stood up for Eve. It was as if God the Father was saying to the serpent, "You mess with My daughter, you mess with *Me*." God lowered the boom on the enemy that day. In essence, He said, "You tried to come between My daughter and Me; now you wait and see. Her offspring is going to be your downfall."

For millennia since then, the enemy has tried frantically to gain a position of power and victory over humanity – over Eve's offspring. After all, every human reflects God to him. Remember, you were made in the image of God (Genesis 1:27), so when the enemy sees you, it reminds him of the One who declared his defeat. Also remember, the enemy knows the power of God's words. He knows that God created the entire world simply by speaking words with His mouth (Genesis 1). He had to know that day in the garden that he was doomed as soon as the words left the Father's mouth. But now, not only has his defeat been declared, it has been accomplished through Jesus' death on the Cross and His resurrection (Colossians 2:15). So now the enemy resorts to trying to make all of God's sons and daughters (who also happen to be Eve's offspring) forget the victory Jesus achieved for us.

1 Corinthians 15:22 says, "For as in Adam all die, so in Christ all will be made alive." While we don't see an image of Jesus standing in front of Eve, offering her

Grace in person like He did to Mary Magdalene, the woman caught in adultery, and the woman at the well, we do see that He carried out Eve's redemption exactly as God the Father decreed that day in the Garden. Eve was the mother of all people (Genesis 3:20), so Jesus was in fact, her seed, her offspring. Jesus carried out the defeat of the enemy that had been spoken by God the Father thousands of years before. Once and for all, He settled the score against the serpent, the one who dared to deceive and use His beloved daughter, the one who tried to turn the Father against the daughter. The serpent's plan failed miserably and backfired dramatically on the day when Jesus made retribution for Eve's sin; on that day, instead of punishing Eve, He punished the enemy himself.

Today, God your Father is offering you the same victory and restoration that He gave to Eve. Maybe you've suffered some deep, horrible consequences because of your own bad choices or because of a predator's deception and abuse of you. God wants you to know that you're still His daughter. He still loves you more than you can imagine. And He wants you to know that He has already settled the score between the real enemy, who dared to mess with you, His beloved daughter. Your Father is standing here, ready to protect you and cover you and hide you in His shadow, safe from all harm.

And what about all those loved ones your sin hurt in the process? Just remember, it was Eve's offspring, Jesus, who has now done what needed to be done to redeem *all* of mankind – to redeem all of Eve's kids for every generation the earth has ever and will ever see. Not one person was left out of God's redemptive plan. God will take care of your loved ones, too. The same God who can heal *your* heart can heal *theirs*. Trust Him and accept His Love for both you and all of those you love.

There is much we can learn from this little trip through the Bible, but I hope that above all, you can see that these women were very obviously chosen and loved by God, in spite of their circumstances and life choices.

Just think: We just covered the full spectrum, from the virgin to the woman caught in adultery, from the innocent orphan to the demon-possessed woman, from the mother of all mankind to the stereotyped woman with five failed marriages.

Surely you can find yourself somewhere in between all of that. Surely you can see that the Father loves all of His daughters, and you are no exception! Remember the two things we learned about a true father: He loves all of His children the same, and His Love is never swayed by our actions.

So why did we spend so much time examining all of this? We took our time here, because in order for you to see yourself for who you really are, you have to understand and embrace your identity as a daughter of the all-powerful, all-loving God. You have to be able to see yourself through the eyes of your Father. And to do that, you have to understand the heart of your Father.

We can never truly understand love the way God intended it to exist between two people, unless we understand the Love that exists between God and us. If we can begin to grasp and grow in *that* Love, we will find so much security in Him that we can then recognize when a man is (or isn't) presenting us with the promise of true love.

Chapter Five
MEET TRUE LOVE

Sadly, we tend to have a distorted view of Love. The movies teach us that love is blind, that love is spur-of-the-moment, that love captures us forcefully and unexpectedly, causing us to do things we never planned to do. Culture swears that love sometimes leads you through agony, addiction, and pain, and that you can't help whom you fall in love with. We are constantly bombarded with ideas of love and romance that, while they may make us feel butterflies in our stomachs, are not true representations of the picture the Bible paints of True Love.

WHAT LOVE IS (AND WHAT LOVE ISN'T)

Our romantic notions of love may make us feel warm and fuzzy when we're watching our favorite chick-flick, but unfortunately, we have subconsciously bought into a lot of myths about love that set us up for relationship failure. The warm and fuzzies often evolve into unrealistic expectations we project onto other human beings, forgetting they are just as imperfect and fallible as we are. For our own sake and the sake of others in our lives, let us dismantle these myths and embrace the truth about Love.

Truth 1: Love is not an emotion. Love is a decision, which will inevitably affect the emotions.

It's okay to be emotional. We just can't trust our emotions to be the Love Thermometer for us, telling us when it's really "True Love" that we're feeling for someone. Our emotional thermometers bounce up and down like a yo-yo, sometimes getting stuck at the bottom and just spinning us in circles until we're dizzy and can't think clearly. Emotions are kind of like that one crazy family member who is the life of the party at every get-together, but she can't seem to make a wise relationship or career decision if her life depended on it. We still love her as much as we love the rest of the family; we want to keep her around, but if we're smart, we aren't going to go to her for serious advice. Similarly, we need to appreciate and embrace our emotions; they are a valuable part of who we are, so don't kick them out of the party! Just don't trust them to let you know when it's True Love that you're experiencing.

We spend a lot of time wondering what Love *feels* like. But aren't we glad God's Love for us doesn't waver with His emotions? *Wait... God has emotions?* Of course, He does! Remember, we were made in His image. We feel, because He feels. And just in case we are ever tempted to think God can't relate to how we feel, Hebrews tells us this about Jesus: "This High Priest of ours understands our weaknesses, for he faced all of the same testings we do, yet he did not sin" (Hebrews 4:15 NLT).

We see throughout Scripture that God *feels,* often in response to our actions and choices. Take a look at a few examples:

1. God feels grief and sorrow.

And do not grieve the Holy Spirit of God ... Get rid of all bitterness, rage and anger, brawling and slander, along with every form of malice (Ephesians 4:30 – 31).

Jesus told His disciples, "My soul is crushed with grief to the point of death..." (Matthew 26:38 NLT).

2. God feels anger.

In John 2:13 – 25, we see Jesus become angry when He finds merchants in the temple who are using the sacred place of worship as a glorified marketplace for their own business endeavors. In fact, there are many instances in Scripture when God becomes angry. Anger is an emotion we have all felt, probably more than we'd like. As it turns out, God feels it, too.

3. God feels delight.

For the Lord delights in his people... (Psalm 149:4 NLT).

The Lord your God is with you... He will take great delight in you... (Zephaniah 3:17).

God is certainly a God who *feels.* Surely I have done many things in my life that have saddened Him. Surely I have caused Him disappointment and probably even grief at times. Thank God that His Love for me isn't based on His emotion; it isn't swayed by how my actions make Him feel each day! The same is true for you. In spite of all the sins you and I would commit, He still gave us those verses in Romans 8:38 – 39, assuring us that nothing – no thing – can separate us from His Love.

God has modeled for us that Love is a decision. He chose to love us. That kind of Love is more powerful than the imposter of emotion that we often confuse for Love. How powerful is your Love for someone if it can be swayed every time they do something that displeases you? How shallow is your commitment to them, if every time your emotions bounce down, you hit the road?

In a very small way, Hollywood sometimes gets it right when the movies portray love that powers through the other person's flaws and mistakes. However, let's bring some balance here, because we need to understand the other side of it, too.

Truth 2: Love isn't blind. Love is aware and protective.

1 Corinthians 13, which is often dubbed "The Love Chapter" of the Bible, gives us a beautiful, poetic description of what True Love does – and doesn't – look like:

> Love is patient, love is kind. It does not envy, it does not boast, it is not proud. It does not dishonor others, it is not self-seeking, it is not easily angered, it keeps no record of wrongs. Love does not delight in evil but rejoices with the truth. It always protects, always trusts, always hopes, always perseveres. Love never fails... (1 Corinthians 13:4-8).

On the surface, it's easy to think that this passage indicates that Love *is* blind. Descriptions like, "patient, kind, not easily angered, keeps no record of wrongs, always perseveres," may make you think that if you're in a relationship, you should stay committed to the relationship no matter what and wait for Love to overcome all the problems. You may read these words and think that no matter how badly he treats you, no matter how unmotivated he is to make something of himself, no matter how low his moral and ethical standards are, you need to stick with it and keep no record of wrongs. Let's dig a little deeper.

While it's true that the Bible calls us to walk in love, forgiveness, and patience with one another (Colossians 3:13; Galatians 5:22), I see nowhere that it calls us to walk in abusive or oppressive relationships. I urge you to look at the full meaning of the passage in 1 Corinthians 13. We often see it as an indicator of the kind of Love we should possess for others, which is true, but keep in mind that 2 Corinthians 6:14 instructs us, "Do not be unequally yoked with unbelievers" (ESV). I want us to focus on the word "unequally." If I am called to offer the kind of Love described in 1 Corinthians 13, then should I not be looking for a life partner who is striving to walk *equally* in this same kind of Love? **While we are called to walk in Love toward all people, we are not called to walk in intimate friendship and relationship with all people.** It's wise to evaluate your close relationships against this description of Love that the Bible gives us.

If you're currently in or are considering a dating relationship with someone who doesn't walk in the 1 Corinthians 13 kind of Love – maybe he doesn't treat you well, he's self-centered, he's indifferent toward you, or he's outright abusive – then I urge you to ask yourself the tough questions and measure the so-called love he offers you against this standard:

> ➢ Is he patient? Is he kind?

> ➢ Is he envious, jealous, boastful, and proud?

> ➤ Does he honor you and others?

> ➤ Is he self-seeking?

> ➤ Is he easily angered?

> ➤ Does he bring up your past mistakes (keep a record of your wrongs)?

> ➤ Does he protect you?

> ➤ Does he trust you?

Perhaps you need to ask these questions about yourself as well; is the relationship inspiring you to grow in this biblical model of Love? Do you find yourself dishonoring others more since you've known him? Do you find yourself self-absorbed, prone to jealousy, or generally impatient with the people around you? What qualities is the relationship bringing out of you?

See, True Love indeed is not blind. I learned this by personal experience. I spent three years thinking I was in love with a young man who, if he reciprocated my affection, never let on that he did. Nonetheless, I felt very strongly that he was "the one," so in the spirit of 1 Corinthians 13 (so I thought), I persevered.

Eventually, we got to be close friends; at least it seemed that way on the surface. We casually hung out almost daily, we both seemed to enjoy each other's company, and I felt like we were finally making progress in getting to know each other better. I couldn't really understand why he didn't pursue a deeper relationship with me, but I was willing to wait it out. After all, *Love never fails,* right? I just knew that at some point my perseverance would pay off.

What I didn't realize until after the fact was that even in the platonic friendship we were building, we weren't cultivating the 1 Corinthians 13 model of Love. I found myself taking on what I now realize were undesirable characteristics that became so engrained in my personality that it has taken years to try to undo them. If I had honestly asked myself the questions posed above, both about him and about me, the answers would not have pointed to a healthy relationship on either side of the equation. To explain, let me fill you in on the turning point of the story.

During the summer of the year we had gotten so close, I went on vacation with my parents and my sister. While we were there, my mom made a simple but eye-opening observation. One afternoon, while we were all back at the hotel for a few minutes, I got a call on my cell phone. It was him. Excited to hear from him while I was on vacation, I answered, and he began telling me about a great idea he had just had. He went on for a while, giving me all the details. Always trying to be supportive, I shared his enthusiasm for the idea. Then I began to tell him a little about our trip so far. I had only gotten a few sentences out when he said, "Yeah, well, I just called to tell you that, so I'll let you go now." After we hung up, Mom very wisely pointed out that he didn't seem very interested in hearing what I had to say; he was only interested in what he called to tell me. The more I thought about it, the more I realized that was a trend in our friendship. He was rarely interested in anything I brought up. Everything revolved around what he did or didn't want. I watched movies I didn't want to watch because he wanted to; we listened to whatever music he was in the mood to hear; we talked about what he wanted to talk about; and we hung out whenever he felt like it. It was never about me, to the point that I was not being true to myself, to my personality, or to my beliefs and dreams anymore.

It was a tough pill to swallow, but I'm glad I did. Remember that phrase that Love *always protects*? What was really happening that day was that Love was protecting me through the words of my mother. When she spoke truth to me that day, it made me realize that what I thought was Love blossoming between him and me was merely a superficial, one-sided friendship. It was convenient for him to be able to call me whenever he needed someone to hang out with or whenever he had a great idea. But he didn't display any of the qualities of 1 Corinthians 13 toward me, even in our friendship.

I knew if he didn't display those qualities in a friendship, he wouldn't display them in a romantic relationship. I decided I had had enough of not being honored, protected, and trusted in this relationship. I had had enough of the self-seeking indifference he displayed toward me. The relationship was no longer worth the investment of my time. So after three intense years of pouring my heart into hopes and dreams that revolved around this guy, I moved on. It wasn't easy, but it was worth it! My Father God carried me through the difficult but freeing process of letting go.

You may be in an unhealthy relationship, either like the one I experienced or maybe even more entangled and more toxic. If you are in a relationship with a man who is willing to violate you physically – and that could be physical abuse or simply sexual gratification – then Love is not prevailing in that relationship. If he talks down to you constantly, Love is not at the center. If he is only ever interested in what he wants and what he needs and never gives you much of a second thought, then Love is not ruling your relationship. If he doesn't do his best to protect you on every level – physically, emotionally, spiritually, and even socially – then it doesn't matter how much you *feel* like you love him or how much he says he loves you. If only one of you is trying to walk in True Love, that is your signal to run, and fast!

If you don't have the courage yet to break free and move on, ask God to help you. You've got a big, powerful Father who lacks nothing in terms of courage and bravery. He can carry you through the transition just like He did for me. You'll be glad you let go and moved on.

> [Side note: I presume that I am talking to unmarried people here. If you are married and your marriage is on the rocks, I am not telling you to leave your spouse, nor am I telling you to remain in a violent or abusive marriage. I urge you to search out the Scriptures and to seek biblical counsel and godly wisdom from your pastor or church leaders to know how to handle your specific situation. If you are in a marriage like this, I pray for God's divine intervention, and I pray for His wisdom, grace, and courage to help you to know how to turn your situation around. Remember, nothing is impossible for Him, and no one is too far for Him to reach.]

Truth 3: Love is not to be fallen into. It is to be entered into reverently and walked out intentionally.

This dovetails off of the first point about Love being a decision, and we will expound more on that now. I think it is important to reiterate the fact that you *do* have a choice about whom you fall in love with!

This isn't to say that you won't have romantic feelings for the person you choose to love. None of what I am saying is intended to strip away our emotions and God-given feelings of attraction that we will have for our future spouses. In fact, I fully expect that romantic attraction will be a factor when my future husband and I begin our journey together. We just have to be aware that Love is much deeper than that, and we have to be deliberate about not letting those feelings rule us and lead us.

Many of us have "fallen" in love so many times that we feel like we have broken every emotional bone in us from all those falls! We set ourselves up for heartbreak and failure when we follow romantic attraction every which way it leads us.

See, the problem with falling in love is that when the feelings change or the relationship hits a rocky place, you can fall right back out of love. If your basis for love is your feelings, then your entire relationship will crash because you never learned how to be intentional about your love for the other person. When we understand True Love, we realize that it must go deeper than attraction; it must involve deliberate commitment to the other person.

You may think I'm crazy here, but I'll throw this out as food for thought. It's interesting that with as much emphasis as our society puts on emotion, physical attraction, and "chemistry" between two people, we often ridicule cultures where marriages are arranged by parents or kingdoms. Don't get me wrong; I am not endorsing the practice of arranged marriage, and I'm personally grateful that my parents didn't subscribe to the idea! However, there is an element of intentionality and decision that many couples have had to discover because they found themselves in arranged marriages, and I think that like them, we can also benefit from understanding the power of a decision.

There's a story in the Bible that beautifully ties together both worlds. Genesis 24 gives us the detailed account of how Abraham commissioned his servant to go and find a wife for his son, Isaac. Think about that. This isn't just a parent arranging a marriage; it's a parent sending his *servant* to find a wife for his son. But Abraham gives the servant specific instructions, and he even tells him that the Lord will send an angel ahead of him to guide him to his son's wife-to-be (v. 7). As far as we know, Isaac has no idea what's transpiring behind the scenes. His dad's servant disappears for a few days; then one day while Isaac is out minding his own business, the servant arrives with a girl, Rebekah, and tells Isaac the whole story (vs. 62 – 66). Now, in our day and culture, Isaac would immediately become indignant, march to his father's tent, and demand to know who Abraham thought he was! He would self-centeredly point out that Abraham had no right to meddle in his life or to dictate that he marry anyone besides whomever he falls in love with on his own! Isaac doesn't do that. Isaac must have had a lot of trust in his father's love for him and in his father's wisdom. We see by his actions that Isaac makes a conscious decision to embrace and receive Rebekah as his wife, and this intentional decision leads to the words we read in the last verse of the chapter, "He loved her deeply..." (v. 67).

In Isaac's case, his intentional decision came first, and that decision led to his falling in love with his wife. Granted, I would say that in our day and age, the chances are that you and I will probably not face the same circumstances Isaac did. I'm not suggesting that you just pick a guy out of a crowd and make a decision to love him. On the contrary, the reason I believe it is important to understand this principle is that, no matter how starry-eyed your future marriage begins, the day will come when the feelings cannot sustain your relationship the way they fueled it in the beginning. Feelings change, and they won't be what they once were. It doesn't mean they will be gone forever, but you may hit a time when you feel like you've fallen out of love with your spouse. In those times, the thing that will carry you and your husband through that season will be the power of your decision to love each other. Your marriage will make it, in spite of the presence or absence of feelings, if your relationship is grounded in a mutual, covenant decision. Your commitment to one another will get you through the tough times when the butterflies aren't there, and it will carry you into an even deeper love with one another than you began with. Like Isaac toward Rebekah, your commitment will cause you both to love one another... *deeply*.

We now understand that Love is not a feeling, Love is not blind, and Love is not meant to be haphazardly fallen into. But before we leave this topic of myth-busting, there's one more, really huge myth I want to dispel in our hearts and minds.

WHO LOVE IS

Here is perhaps the biggest revelation we can possibly have about Love: **Love is not a thing. Love is a Person.**

1 John 4:8 tells us quite plainly, **"God is love"** (NLT).

These three words can forever change your view of Love. All this time, when we thought we were talking about feelings, decisions, emotions, intentions, qualities... What we were really talking about wasn't a "what;" it was a "Who." Love has a name; it's God.

If you can understand that God *is* Love, then suddenly your capability to understand True Love just increased exponentially. Beyond that, your ability to measure your own actions and the actions of others against the standard of True Love will increase as well.

This is why everything rises and falls based on our relationship with God. Our capacity for knowing and giving and receiving Love in our human relationships is directly linked to our knowing Love-in-Person, Jesus Christ. As we grow in our relationship with Him, then we become better equipped to love in all aspects of our lives!

LOVE IN EVERY ASPECT

One thing I've been learning about Love is that, as my understanding of Love increases, my outpouring of Love must increase also. I'll admit that I have been quite selfish at times with extending love to others. I've reserved my love for those closest to me, the ones who have proven their trustworthiness, the ones I can count on. While I have always said I love all people in general (because I felt like that's what the Bible teaches us to do), I've been very stingy about truly extending love to just anyone. I've basically kept it reserved for those closest to me – my family and close friends made the cut, but not just anyone else would.

The more I grow in Love, the more I see the error of my ways. Love must infiltrate every aspect of my life. True Love must be allowed to overflow out of my heart to others, even those who seem not to fit my perfect idea of who is lovable. When I understand how God loved me in spite of all of my sin, filth, dirty thoughts, ignorance, and even this selfishness I'm describing to you now – when I really think about how great His Love for me is – I can't withhold His unconditional love from other people in my life, just because they don't meet my hypocritical standard of loveliness or lovability.

Remember that verse that tells us that God is Love? Well, as it turns out, there's a greater context there that we would do well to consider. I'd like us to take a moment and ponder these words together:

> *Dear friends, let us continue to love one another, for love comes from God. Anyone who loves is a child of God and knows God. But* **anyone who does not love does not know God,** *for God is love.*

> *God showed how much he loved us by sending his one and only Son into the world so that we might have eternal life through him.* **This is real love** *– not that we loved God,*

but that he loved us and sent his Son as a sacrifice to take away our sins.

Dear friends, **since God loved us that much, we surely ought to love each other.** *No one has ever seen God. But* **if we love each other, God lives in us,** *and his love is brought to full expression in us.*

... God is love, and **all who live in love live in God, and God lives in them.** *And as we live in God,* **our love grows more perfect.** *So we will not be afraid on the day of judgment, but we can face him with confidence because we live like Jesus here in this world* (1 John 4:7 – 12, 16 – 17 NLT).

Wow. And just in case that didn't explain it clearly enough, John goes on and spells it out a little more plainly for us:

If someone says, "I love God," but hates a fellow believer, that person is a liar; for if we don't love people we can see, how can we love God, whom we cannot see? And he has given us this command: Those who love God must also love their fellow believers (1 John 4:20 – 21 NLT).

We often call 1 Corinthians 13 "The Love Chapter," but I have to say, I think 1 John 4 is a strong contender for the title. It points us past just the qualities and attributes of Love and smacks us in the face with the fact that, if God's Love is a reality in our lives, it must be poured out onto those around us. We can't live selfishly, resentfully, or bitterly with one another and claim to know God and to know Love.

It's been a process, but I'm learning to let go of the disappointments and let-downs people have handed to me in various situations, to stop punishing new friendships for the failures of old friendships, and to extend Love to other people, regardless of whether or not they fit my textbook definition of being lovable. Ephesians 4:32 says:

> *Instead, be kind to each other, tenderhearted, forgiving one another, just as Christ has forgiven you* (NLT).

I challenge you to join me in walking forward in God's Love, Love that He has so freely given to us with no strings attached. As we continue our journey together, let's choose to offer that same unconditional Love to all of those around us, regardless of how they can or cannot reciprocate it to us. **Let us love, not to be affirmed in return, but simply because Love loves us.**

> *We love because he first loved us.*
> 1 John 4:19

Chapter Six
NOT ALONE BUT ALONE

Loneliness is not a new problem, but let's be honest: It *is* a problem. While we want to be stable, healthy individuals, learning to be content, to like ourselves, and to enjoy quiet moments of solitude, we still battle this constant awareness of being alone. If you're like me, your sustained state of loneliness can drive you to ask a lot of questions about God's plans and intentions for your life. But we all know that loneliness itself is not healthy, nor is it what God intended for us... *Is it?*

Maybe you've wrestled with loneliness and what to do when you find yourself in that miserably desperate place. After all, it's one thing to choose to grab moments of isolation because you need to pull away and be by yourself; it's another thing to be by yourself because you have no choice. Let's look at how to handle those moments when, in spite of trying to love God with all our hearts, we still find ourselves feeling so very... alone.

Personally, I used to struggle with condemnation over feeling lonely, because I believed that if God were really enough for me, I shouldn't be feeling this way. I wrestled with this faulty conclusion for a long time. The stigma of condemnation became implanted in my mind, and I felt even less-equipped to handle periods of loneliness in my life.

Thankfully, God has lifted me out of that place of loneliness, and I want to share with you some of the insights I have gained along the way. Let's deal with two questions that many of us may wrestle with, and then we'll talk about how to kick out loneliness.

Question 1: Does Loneliness Mean God Isn't Enough for Me?

The short answer: No. Now, if you'll trust me for a few minutes here, I want to hold off on the long answer, because it is rooted in the needs and desires we feel for companionship. We're going to delve fully into that later on, and we'll talk about why, if we love God fully, we still feel the need for relationships with other people. However, I think it's important that we confront this issue of loneliness before we dive into those things. So if we can put a pin in this question for a few minutes, we'll return to it and flesh it out in the next chapter.

Question 2: Does Loneliness Mean I Need to Seek God More?

The short answer: Yes. The long answer to this question is where I want us to hang out for a few minutes. The remedy to loneliness is found in our relationship with God. However, we don't need to seek God harder to try to pretend the loneliness isn't there or to try to drown it out. We aren't using God as a bandage to cover up the hurt when we feel lonely. Instead, we're going to learn to be open and honest before the Lord, our loving Father. We're going to open our hearts to Him, let Him know how we're feeling, and let Him lift us out of the loneliness when we find ourselves there.

What does seeking God have to do with loneliness? When our relationship with God is a real *relationship* – one in which we communicate, we walk and talk together, and we live life together – then we will find that we are never actually alone. As the psalmist says, God is our Number One Refuge in times of trouble:

> *God is our refuge and strength, an ever-present help in trouble* (Psalm 46:1).

I think loneliness counts as a time of trouble; it troubles our hearts and our minds, leaving us feeling restless, anxious, or even desperate and in despair. Therefore, we need to be sure that in those times, our Father God is the first one we turn to for help.

If you find yourself always turning first to your friends, social media, the social scene in your town, or whatever your go-to loneliness remedy may be, you are crippling yourself spiritually. In fact, you're running the risk of wasting the purpose of Single for your life. That's not to say you don't need your friends or that there's not a legitimate place for social interaction in your life. You do need friends, and you do need a social life in some way or another. You just need to remember to make God your first go-to. When we start with Him, a few things happen:

1. **We are no longer co-dependent on other people.** Have you ever known a very needy person? Have you ever *been* that very needy person? When we are needy, our own needs for affirmation convert into an emotional drain to the people around us, sometimes even to the people we love most. Despite our best intentions, we exhaust our family or friends' supply of

support, advice, and availability toward us. This happens commonly when we don't know how to turn to God first to meet our needs. Unfortunately, needy friends make needy spouses. So we would do well to let God work this neediness out of us now, while we're in Single! Now, don't get me wrong; I'm not saying we don't need people; we absolutely do need other people in our lives! God puts us in each other's lives to help support and sharpen one another (Proverbs 27:17). But if we can make a habit of *starting* with God in times of trouble, then we will learn more and more how to pull from His unending supply of strength and affirmation. Our friendships will benefit as a result.

2. **We prepare ourselves for healthy futures.** In our minds, the immediate fix for loneliness is companionship – right now! But in reality, there are a lot of people trapped in very lonely marriages. Many people have discovered that when two incomplete people get married, it does not equal a whole, complete person on either side. Two incomplete people make an incomplete marriage. As a result, a lot of people are sitting in marriages that feel every bit as lonesome as you feel right now in Single. By learning to turn to God first, we allow Him to build us into healthy, whole individuals, and we'll be much better-prepared for the road ahead, whatever it entails!

3. **We build trust in our relationship with God.** The more we turn to Him first, the more we will see Him meeting our deep, inner needs. We will recognize more and more that He indeed is the loving Father we talked

about earlier, that He cares about our every longing, and that He wants to be involved in every aspect of our lives. He even wants to be involved in lifting us out of loneliness. That kind of trust in a relationship is priceless, and it will carry us for a lifetime to come.

NEVER ALONE

Let's go back to that verse in Psalms again: "God is our refuge and strength, an ever-present help in trouble." The key word here is "ever-present." Ever. Present. Think about it. Loneliness is when you feel like you're all by yourself, with no one else *present.* But here we see that God is ever-present. He is always there. He is always *here.*

Even though I know the moments will come when the need for human companionship is great, when it's pulling on our emotions and our heartstrings, we must remember that God is right here with us, even if we don't feel Him at that moment. I know it's hard to grasp when we can't see Him in front of us, but it doesn't change how very real His Presence is. In these moments, we can press closer to Him; we can allow Him to be our companion. When we learn to press into God instead of seeking fulfillment in shallow alternatives, we will develop a depth in our relationship with God now – here in Single – that we will carry with us the rest of our lives.

What do I mean by "press into God?" Just imagine a little kid who has fallen and scraped her knee; it may be only a minor cut, or maybe it's a deep gash. See her as she leaves all of her friends on the playground and runs to her Daddy, who has been watching her from a bench nearby. She falls into his open arms, crying uncontrollably, and lets him tend to her wound. He lifts her onto his lap, and she buries her head in his chest, letting him hold her tightly until she feels brave enough to go back and play with the other kids again. She knows Daddy is always right there, but there are certain times when she needs to *press into* him to let him tell her everything will be okay. Your Father God is always here with you, but there are times when you will need to shut out all the other things competing for your attention and really *press* into Him. Let Him tell you everything is okay. Remind yourself of His promises and His Love for you. Let Him make everything better. Let Him hold you and wipe the tears away.

There are things that God wants to work in us (and some things He wants to work out of us) – there are opportunities for spiritual and personal growth that come only by spending time with Him – but it takes our time and attention. Even though Single is a temporary season for us, it *is* the season in which we have resources of time and focus that we may not have as abundantly down the road. If we don't give God our full devotion now, if we don't turn to Him in our loneliness during Single, what makes us think we will turn to Him when we hit a rough spot in our marriage? Are we naïve enough to think that once we're married, we'll never have problems anymore?

If we waste the opportunities we have right now in Single, it would be like our friend Evan parking that shiny new bike in a corner of his room and passing it day after day, year after year, without getting on and riding... all because he's waiting until he turns 16 and can have a car. Ignoring the opportunities in front of us will not help expedite the process God wants to lead us through. Ignoring these opportunities will only make us less-prepared for the seasons ahead.

HOW DO I SEEK GOD WHEN I'M LONELY?

But seek first his kingdom and his righteousness,
and all these things will be given to you as well.
Matthew 6:33

As I write these words today, please allow me to be transparent with you. At this very moment I am experiencing some of the longing, aloneness, and even boredom that we singles can feel. It is a Sunday evening, all of today's busyness has subsided, and I found myself sort of wandering through the house trying to figure out how I want to spend these last few hours of my weekend. I caught myself thinking just a few minutes ago, "If I had a man, I wouldn't be this bored." But then I had to take those thoughts into captivity to the obedience of Christ (2 Corinthians 10:5).

Why do I tell you these things? So that you will understand that this is something we *walk* out in Christ. It's not an open and shut case. Our focus, longings, and desires do not just pop into line with the snap of a finger. We have to actively apply the principles of God, the Word of God, and the promises of God to our daily thought processes. This is actually a wonderful opportunity for us. If we learn to take control over our desires and thoughts in this area of loneliness, how much more we will be able to rule over our desires and thoughts in other areas of life, throughout the entire course of our lives!

So I decided to write more to you today, even to help *me* overcome right now! When I sat down to write, the phrase came to me, "Righteousness, peace, and joy in the Holy Ghost..." (see Romans 14:17). What an appropriate truth for Christian singles to focus on! Walking out this life of purity and self-control, of diligence and focus requires:

> ➢ Righteousness: character, integrity, and relationship with God.

> ➢ Peace that surpasses our understanding and all of our questions of "Why?" and "Why not?" and "Why not now?"

> ➢ Joy in the Holy Spirit, which is found in God's Presence.

According to Romans 14, these are three elements of the kingdom of God. No wonder Jesus instructed us to seek first the *kingdom* of God. He said that then all these things - the fulfillment of our needs, plans, and desires - will be *added* to us. We find our completion and our value in the kingdom of God. That is why Jesus said these things will be "added;" He knows that as we seek the fundamentals of the kingdom of God – righteousness, peace, and joy - these building blocks of abundant life become part of us. *He completes us.* **Then the things of this life can be added to us without subtracting anything from us.**

When we seek after the things of this life before seeking the kingdom of God, we shape our lives and our value by those things, creating a false sense of identity and security; then we attempt to "add" the kingdom of God to the picture. It just doesn't work that way. The kingdom has to be first.

Think about it this way. You may love to accessorize your outfits. Maybe you love scarves or shoes or purses, or maybe your philosophy is the more bling, the better! However, your accessories hold very little use if the outfit isn't in place first. Let's think about it literally. If you don't put on the jeans and shirt, then all your accessories do is draw more attention to your exposed self. No amount of necklaces and shoes can substitute for the clothes themselves! Accessories are meant to *add to* the beauty of the outfit, to enhance something that is already functioning without them. They aren't meant to replace the garments!

The things of this life are like useless accessories without the kingdom of God being properly established in our lives first. On their own, those things will leave us empty, emotionally raped, and devalued when we try to use them as substitutes for God Himself. However, when they are *added to* the life of someone who is already seeking God first, then they are beautiful, balanced elements of life! They are fulfilling and even enhance our identities and the various facets that make up each of us as an individual. In proper order, they are being added as accessories to someone who already knows that her strength, grace, and value are built on the solid, unshakable foundation of God's kingdom; she is already fully clothed in righteousness, peace, and joy in the Holy Ghost!

When we find ourselves wrestling face-to-face with loneliness, we need to make a conscious decision to defeat it by pursuing God first! We can follow Jesus' instruction to seek first God's kingdom, refocusing our hearts and lives on each of these areas. Let's jump in!

HOW TO SEEK RIGHTEOUSNESS

1. **Ask God to lead you.** Psalm 5:8 says: "Lead me, Lord, in your righteousness... make your way straight before me."

2. **Evaluate your current habits,** and ask God to show you if anything you are engaging in is not lining up with His standard of righteousness. If you realize that you're making choices that go against His Word, then admit that to Him and ask His forgiveness. David's prayer of repentance in Psalm 51 is a great example of how a child of God, having realized their sin, can repent humbly and ask for a new start:

   > *Have mercy on me, O God, according to your unfailing love... Wash away all my iniquity and cleanse me from my sin... Against you, you only, have I sinned... Create in me a pure heart, O God, and renew a steadfast spirit within me... Restore to me the joy of your salvation...* (Psalm 51:1–12).

3. **Remind yourself** that walking in righteousness is accepting God's protection over your life. Proverbs 13:6 says, "Righteousness guards the person of integrity, but wickedness overthrows the sinner."

4. **Know that God does not withhold righteousness** from anyone who asks. Jesus said, "Blessed are those

who hunger and thirst for righteousness, for they will be filled" (Matthew 5:6).

5. **Offer yourself daily to God**, to live out His plans for you that day, to be led by His Spirit in every way.

> *Do not offer any part of yourself to sin as an instrument of wickedness, but rather offer yourselves to God as those who have been brought from death to life; and offer every part of yourself to him as an instrument of righteousness* (Romans 6:13).

6. **Remember that ultimately, righteousness is not about your ability** to do good works and live up to God's standards. Righteousness is a gift from God that you receive through faith in Jesus Christ. "This righteousness is given through faith in Jesus Christ to all who believe" (Romans 3:22).

HOW TO SEEK PEACE

1. **Tell God what you need.** Be open and honest before Him, pouring your heart out to Him. Just be sure not to get bogged down here in your needs, because the next part is essential...

2. **Find things to thank God for.** Make a thankfulness list. You think I'm kidding? How often do we find ourselves wallowing in self-pity over loneliness, when in reality, God has blessed us with so much?! What can you be thankful for today? The roof over your head?

The food in your stomach? The family you do have? A trusted friend? Make a list, and every time you start to feel restless in loneliness, pull that list out and start thanking God – out loud if you have to – for everything on your thankfulness list. What does that have to do with peace? I'm glad you asked.

> ...*Tell God what you need, and **thank him for all he has done. Then you will experience God's peace, which exceeds anything we can understand.** His peace will guard your hearts and minds as you live in Christ Jesus* (Philippians 4:6 – 7 NLT).

Wow! Our peace level is directly linked to our gratitude level. Then, God's peace turns around and acts as a guard, a protector, over our hearts and minds! You may want to take some time and just think about that for a few minutes before moving on.

3. **Understand that you can have peace even when situations aren't peaceful.** A different translation of verse 7 above says, "the peace of God, which passeth all understanding..." (KJV). If you will, think about those express elevators that some hotels and skyscrapers have. You know, the ones that don't even stop at the first twenty floors or so; they don't even waste time dropping off and picking up people on those levels. Some of them are so "express" that they only go straight from the lobby to the penthouse. Now think about the peace of God as an express elevator in your mind. It bypasses all of the hang-ups and delays in your mind –

your own logic, your human understand'
details of your situation – and it takes p(
through you, from head to toe, regardless ѹ
circumstances you're facing. I like to call it the peace
that doesn't make sense! It's the peace you can have
when the doctor gives you a negative diagnosis. It's the
peace you can have in the middle of family arguments.
It's the peace you can have when the world around you
is in chaos. And it's the peace you can have when,
physically, you're alone, but spiritually, you are not
lonely. It's God's Peace Express, and it comes directly
from your ongoing conversation with Him.

4. **Keep the conversation open.** Whether it's your
needs or your thanks, constantly keep your heart open
to God, talking with Him throughout your day as you
would your best friend. Be aware that He is always with
you – ever present – at all times, and even if you're in a
place where you can't open your mouth and speak
words out loud to Him, your spirit can still speak to His
Spirit. This is how you will walk out 1 Thessalonians
5:16 – 18:

> *Always be joyful. Never stop praying. Be thankful*
> *in all circumstances, for this is God's will for you*
> *who belong to Christ Jesus* (NLT).

HOW TO SEEK JOY

1. **Understand that joy is found in God's Presence.**
Psalm 16:11 says, "in your presence there is fullness of
joy" (ESV). There's an added benefit to joy, too.

make it on our own, and it makes us confident, powerful women of God who are able to make a difference in the world around us.

4. **His Spirit is His Presence with us.** Remember the phrase from Romans 14 that started this whole discussion, "righteousness, peace, and joy in the Holy Spirit"? There's a reason "in the Holy Spirit" rounds out the whole thing. When Jesus was preparing His disciples for His departure from earth, He knew they would have some anxiety about not having Him there in the flesh anymore, walking with them day-in and day-out. So He told them these words:

> *But I tell you the truth, it is to your advantage that I go away; for if I do not go away, the Helper (Comforter, Advocate, Intercessor – Counselor, Strengthener, Standby) will not come to you; but if I go, I will send Him (the Holy Spirit) to you [to be in close fellowship with you]"* (John 16:6–7 AMP).

Jesus knew that in the flesh, He could only be with a certain number of people and only at certain times. But He also knew that when the Holy Spirit came, He could fill the life of each and every believer, walking with us always, helping us in every situation. The Holy Spirit is God, ever present with us in every moment of every day.

This model of seeking God's kingdom first, of seeking His righteousness, peace, and joy in the Holy Spirit, will help us to combat loneliness and push it further and further from our lives. Not only will it help now during Single, but it will help us form patterns of communicating with God throughout each day, walking with Him more and more closely. These patterns will become engrained in us and will follow us our entire lives.

As we move forward, I hope to encourage you with this: No matter how lonely we may feel in a moment, we can always remember that, indeed, we are never, ever alone.

Alone, but I'm not lonely
There's One who walks beside me
In front and all-surrounding
His Presence, yes, it guides me.

He knows my deepest longings
He authored them inside me
So when I may feel lonely
His loving arms, they hide me.

I caught a glimpse, so simply
His face—to me, He's looking
With eyes focused intently
Into my soul, He sees.

His passion, it's breathtaking
This King, He loves so deeply
And now, the one He's shaping
Is the single, lonely—me.

My heart responds with, "Yes!"
Lord, my everything is Yours!
My dreams, desires, my best
Into Your hands I pour.

For if I cannot trust You
With the things that I hold near
How will You ever trust me
With the ones that You hold dear?

Father, let my heart beat
To the rhythm of Your plans
Clear my eyes to freely see
How I can be Your hands.

May loneliness no longer be
Companion here to me
Now that Love has set me free
Your captive may I be.

Chapter Seven
TO BE OR NOT TO BE

This is one of the big questions among Christian singles, so it seems. *Is it God's will for me to get married one day, or does He want me to remain single forever?*

In my experience, we Christians who are single often waver between desire for God and desire for our future spouses. As I shared with you earlier, I've personally fought much condemnation from thinking that my desire to be married somehow reflected a weakness in my satisfaction with God. After all, Jesus did instruct us to "Love the Lord your God with all your heart..." (Mark 12:30). For as long as I can remember, I've tried to do exactly that. Even in my sincere devotion to God, however, I found myself second-guessing my desire for a husband in light of my relationship with God. I mean, as far as I could tell, "all" means "all," right? So my hang-up became this constant wondering of how, if I really loved God with *all* my heart, I could still feel the intense need for long-term companionship and love from a human. It seemed only logical that these desires must indicate a lack of fulfillment in God; perhaps I didn't truly love Him with all my heart like I thought I did. The bottom line was I felt guilty about desiring marriage.

To make matters more difficult, there is one particular passage in the Bible that seemed to reinforce my feelings. While I absolutely love the Apostle Paul – his revelations, his frankness, and his passionate love for Jesus – he penned some words that contributed to my internal anxiety. I just couldn't wrap my head around his remarks on marriage in 1 Corinthians 7:

But I wish everyone were single, just as I am. Yet each person has a special gift from God, of one kind or another. So I say to those who aren't married and to widows—it's better to stay unmarried, just as I am. But if they can't control themselves, they should go ahead and marry. It's better to marry than to burn with lust (1 Corinthians 7:7-9 NLT).

Now, maybe these words don't bother you, but they were a huge problem for me. Having strong overachiever tendencies, I'm wired to want to be the best, do the best, and have the best. Always striving to *give* my best to God, this passage generated a lot of turmoil I couldn't seem to resolve. To a very literal thinker, Paul's words evoked these kinds of thoughts in me:

> ➢ *I want all God has for me, God's very* best; *I want to give God* all *of me,* my *very best.*

> ➢ *Paul says it is* better *to stay unmarried, so if I want God's* best, *does that mean I need to stay single?*

> ➢ *Does getting married mean I'd be settling for less than God's best? Is marriage God's consolation prize for someone who just can't stand to stay single?*

> ➢ *Does this mean that because I want to get married one day, I must be consumed with lust?*

> ➢ *If I get married, will I not be able to serve God wholeheartedly anymore?*

The inner tension was real. I wanted more than anything to please God, but I felt from these verses that simply by desiring marriage, I was not giving God as much of me as I should. After all, it sounds like Paul is saying that to marry is to lack self-control and the ability to resist lust and temptation. It sounds as if marriage is the lesser of two callings. How then do I reconcile my absolute love for God with my desire to marry? I didn't realize it then, but I was walking in a lot of fear about my relationship with God. I was afraid I wasn't giving Him enough of me, and I was becoming dreadfully suspicious that this secret, nagging fear was true: *What if, in order for me to have God's best, God wants to keep me single forever?*

Maybe you've dealt with similar questions in one way or another. No matter what angle these fears come from, they can be real problems in the minds of God's daughters.

We asked ourselves in the previous chapter if loneliness means that God isn't enough for us. I gave you the short answer: No, feeling lonely does not mean that God isn't enough. It is an opportunity, like we discussed, to seek God and draw closer to Him. Now that we have a better understanding of how to deal with loneliness itself, let's return to the underlying question and explore the long answer.

Having a deep desire for human companionship is not an indication that you haven't allowed God to be enough for you. How do I know this? I know it, because God gave us both the desire and the *need* for companionship, first with Him, and then with other human beings. Did you catch that? The desires and the need we're feeling for a husband, those originated from God Himself. Not convinced? Let me show you.

GOD CREATED A NEED

Let's go all the way back to the beginning of the human race, and let's look at when God had just created the first human being, a man named Adam.

Adam, freshly created and brought to life by God Himself, is in the Garden of Eden. God has given him authority and dominion over all the other created things, and God Himself personally talks with Adam (Genesis 2:15 – 17). I can imagine Adam walking with God, completely in awe of this thing called life. Maybe God has given him a personal tour of this beautiful, perfect habitat, showing him each and every detail of intricate beauty He has just created. At one point, God brings all of the animals to Adam, and Adam gets the privilege of naming each creature (vs. 19 – 20). What a life, huh? Here's Adam and his Dad – God Himself – hanging out together, not a care in the world.

Now, consider this about brand-new Adam: Adam has never even seen a woman, so he doesn't know what he's missing by not having a wife. Sin has not yet wriggled its way into the human race, so Adam doesn't struggle with lust. And he is hanging out with God on a regular basis, so it's not like he knows what it means to be lonely. Life is good. It's Adam and God, best friends in the Garden. How could anyone ask for a more perfect relationship with God?

In the middle of this very perfect relationship, a sneaky little verse pops up that we often either overlook or misunderstand. But it's there to clue us into something God has brewing behind the scenes. See, just when everything appears to be complete and perfect, the Creator isn't done creating.

> The LORD God said, "It is not good for the man to be alone. I will make a helper suitable for him" (Genesis 2:18).

Hold on. God has been creating one thing after another, and we see in Genesis 1 that at the end of every day, God looks at what He has made and sees that it is *good*. But in Genesis 2:18, God says something entirely different. He says, "It is not good…" Wait. Here in His perfect world, how could anything be *not good?* God speaks and says, "It is not good for the man to be alone." Right there. That. That's where God created the need for companionship in the human race, and more specifically, that's where He created the need for marriage.

See, we often misunderstand God's words here as being a statement of realization or worse, an admission of imperfection in the man He just created. We read this verse and get the impression that God sits back, looks at all He has created, then, suddenly leaning forward to take a better look, scratches His head and says, "Oops! Oh no, we didn't plan on the man feeling lonely! This isn't good… We need to come up with a solution!" We get this mental image of a mopey, forlorn Adam sulking around the Garden, when it dawns on God that Adam is pitifully alone. Seriously, though, is that even possible? Has it ever occurred to you that nothing occurs to God? How can the all-knowing One have a new realization? He can't. He sees all and knows all light-years before we do. And, by the way, He doesn't make mistakes.

We forget that God has just masterfully *created* the entire world. He's just created light, the sun and moon, plants, birds, fish – the whole world as we know it – and how did He do it? With His *words*. God spoke, and the world lined up with His words. He said, "Let there be light," and there was light (Genesis 1:3 KJV). We would be wise to learn this about God's words: **God's words are never comments of realization; they are always creative directions, telling His Creation what to do next.**

When God spoke to Adam, He was not admitting a mistake or flaw. He did not see a lonely man and reluctantly decide to give him a companion as a result. Eve was not God's courtesy gesture to try to apologize for the mistake. God looked at Adam, the perfect man created in His own image, and He *spoke* with the same creative authority that made light. He spoke the words, "It is not good for the man to be alone." In that moment, God with His own words purposefully placed a need inside of the man for a wife. He set a law in motion that has governed humanity ever since, and that law states that it is not good for us to be alone; we were created for covenant relationship, both with God and with another human.

Don't you think that God could have looked at Adam and declared something else? God could have said, "Man shall rule independently and self-sufficiently." God didn't do that. Instead, God created a need. He gave the man the *need* for a wife. He gave it as a gift, not as a point of bondage and not as a curse of loneliness. He gave it, because God knew at that moment the beauty that marriage would be, the power of unity that a man and wife would hold.

Now, you may be asking, *So are you saying that everyone is supposed to get married? What if I don't want to get married? What if I want to stay single all my life?* No, I am absolutely not saying that everyone is supposed to get married, and I believe the Apostle Paul's words are proof of that. I am simply making the point that the need that many of us feel for a future spouse originated with God.

Even if you do not desire to get married, you still have a need for other people, for meaningful relationships in your life. No one is called to walk through life alone. Even the Apostle Paul, happy and grateful for his singleness, was surrounded by and networked with people everywhere. He had trusted companions, ministry partners, and disciples in the Lord. So while not everyone will require a spouse to carry out God's plans and purposes, we all need to realize that we need relationships with other people. If you have any doubts, the writer of Ecclesiastes explains it perfectly:

> *Two are better than one, because they have a good return for their labor: If either of them falls down, one can help the other up. But pity anyone who falls and has no one to help them up ... Though one may be overpowered, two can defend themselves. A cord of three strands is not easily broken* (Ecclesiastes 4:9 – 12).

God clearly wants us to have strong, reliable friendships in this life – "As iron sharpen iron, so one person sharpens another" (Proverbs 27:17) – and for many of us, He also gave us the need for a spouse. In either case, we can rest assured that He knows our needs, and those needs came from Him.

You would think this would be enough to allay my fears and convince me that God gave me the desire for marriage, right? But just in case it wasn't, God showed me another little tidbit of Truth to help knock the guilt out of my mind. Hold on, because this one is pretty literal, and you might even find it a bit comical (I know I do):

> *So God created human beings in his own image... Then God blessed them and said, "Be fruitful and multiply..."* (Genesis 1:27-28 NLT).

One thing that is quite clear in the Bible is that God created sex for marriage only. The Bible clearly defines sex outside of marriage as sin. One day, as I was wrestling with Paul's words from 1 Corinthians 7, it dawned on me: God told Adam and Eve to be fruitful and multiply. Um... There's only one way to do that, *literally*, that is... and there's only one context that God endorses that in – marriage!

It was as if God was saying to me (lightheartedly perhaps), "Okay, if you're not going to believe Me, think about it this way." Hello! If God didn't want us to get married - if His "better" plan was for us all to stay single forever and love Him as single people - then what is His plan for populating the earth? Of course, God would not command us to be fruitful and multiply, only to turn around and say that we all would do better to remain single as the Apostle Paul was! I hope you're laughing at me right now, because I am!

That's how God convinced me that there was a greater context behind Paul's words than just the literal, surface meaning I was inferring from them. God has created some of us who, like

Paul, will remain single all of our lives, will delight in it, and will be in His perfect plan for our lives. He has also created many of us who will get married, will delight in it, and will also be in His perfect plan for our lives.

So that settled a huge issue for me. But then the question remained, and perhaps you'll relate more to this question: *How do I know which category I fall into, the single-forever side or the to-be-married side?*

The secret, underlying fear that haunts many of us singles is this: *What if I want to be married, but God really wants me to stay single forever?*

GOD CREATED A DESIRE

The desire of the righteous ends only in good...
Proverbs 11:23

To answer this question, let's talk for a few minutes about the desires of our hearts. Desires can be a tricky thing, because depending on who or what you are submitted to, your desires can be either godly and pure or sinful and wicked. Paul teaches us clearly:

> *Those who live according to the flesh have their minds set on what the flesh desires; but those who live in accordance with the Spirit have their minds set on what the Spirit desires* (Romans 8:5).

Unfortunately, I can't tell you which side of that verse you fall on. But if you are following after God, living by His Spirit, then the rest of this chapter is for you.

The world says you should follow every desire and every whim. On the contrary, the church oftentimes seems to preach that you should avoid every desire, that desire equals lust or gluttony or some kind of fleshly sin. I find both extremes to be wrong. Let's see what God says about desires.

> *Delight yourself also in the Lord, And He shall give you the desires of your heart* (Psalm 37:4 NKJV).

The word "give" means several different things. First, it can mean *to put, to bestow, to entrust, to appoint.* Second, it can mean *to grant, to yield, to produce.*[1]

I believe this verse has a dual-meaning. We often think of it only in terms of God's *fulfilling* our desires, but we just read that if we walk after the Spirit, our desires will actually line up with His desires. Now we see in Psalm 37:4 that when we delight in the Lord, He *gives* us our hearts' desires. I believe God is involved in the entire process, and here's how:

1. **First, God *gives* us the desires of our heart,** just like He gave Adam the need for companionship; He *bestows* the desires upon us. He *puts* the desires there in the first place, and He does so purposefully – He *appoints* them to carry out His will in our lives. Does that mean that every desire I ever have is from Him? No, because I still make decisions daily to follow the Spirit and not my fleshly (previously sinful) nature. Don't confuse desires with temptations.

   James 1:14 says, "Temptation comes from our own desires, which entice us and drag us away" (NLT). We need to understand that the word "desires" in this verse is different than the word "desires" in Psalm 37:4. The word James uses for the desires that lead us to temptation means *lust* or *desire for what is forbidden*.[2] In contrast, the word for "desires" in Psalm 37:4 means, *a request* or *petition*.[3]

If we're following God, seeking Him first, we can trust that He is depositing the desires in us that He wants us to have, and we can also ask Him to reveal to us by His Spirit if there are any desires in us that did not originate with Him. I love the raw openness of David when he pleads with God, "Search me, O God, and know my heart! Try me and know my thoughts! And see if there be any grievous way in me, and lead me in the way everlasting!" (Psalm 139:23 – 24 ESV).

2. **Second, God *gives* us the desires of our hearts!**
   Now that we've submitted our desires to Him, we delight in Him, and we're following after the Spirit, we can joyfully and confidently expect Him to *fulfill* the desires He's given us! We trust Him to *grant* them to us. See, after God puts the desires in us, He then takes it upon Himself to fulfill those same desires. How great is that?! It's just like we saw with Adam: God spoke the need for companionship, and then followed it up by fulfilling the need He had just created in the man.

   The caveat for us today lies in God's timing. He doesn't always fulfill the desire as quickly as we wish He would! And it's easy, in our own limited thinking, to be tempted to ask God, *Why did You give me the desire in the first place, only to withhold it from me?* I am finding, as much as it goes against my own tendency to be impatient, that the gap between the time God gives us a desire (creates it) and gives us the desire (fulfills it) is a very valuable period of growth and preparation – if we'll let it be.

We quickly get impatient when God makes us wait a year or two or five or ten longer than we wanted, but think about Abraham. Genesis 12 tells us that when the Lord told Abraham (then called Abram) to leave his home country, He promised to make him into a great nation. The first obvious requirement for this to happen was offspring; this promise required children who could then have children and so on. Yet when he acted on this word from God and left his home, Abraham was 75 years old, and his wife had never been able to have children (Genesis 12:1 – 4). When he was 99 years old, God spoke to him again and reminded him that He hadn't forgotten the promise (the desire) He gave to Abraham many years before. During this conversation, the Lord told Abraham that Sarah would give birth to a son. Sarah was already 90 years old, and even if she hadn't been barren all her life, she was well beyond childbearing years. But God insisted that His promise would come true just as He had said (Genesis 17:1 – 22). Genesis 21 confirms that God fulfilled the promise He made. When Abraham was 100 years old, Sarah gave birth to their son, Isaac.

Abraham waited 25 years from the time God told him he

would become a great nation until the *first* tangible sight of God's fulfilling that promise: the moment he held his and Sarah's son in his arms. And we think we've waited a long time for God to bring us our husbands!

We don't always understand God's timing, but we still would be wise to trust it. Remember what we learned about the heart of our Father; it is His delight to give us good gifts! He is not going to give us desires only to withhold them out of cruelty or punishment. If He hasn't fulfilled the promise yet, it's because He has a greater reason in mind than you or I know – and I guarantee you, that reason is for our own good!

Now that we have this foundation of understanding and trust, let's lay to rest the question of, *Does God want me to be single forever?*

Ask yourself this question instead: *Do I desire to be single forever?* If your answer is, "Yes," then that's awesome, and I know you will enjoy the road of Single! However, if your answer is, "No," then the chances are that God doesn't want you to be single forever, either.

I truly believe that if we have submitted our entire lives to Him, including our hearts, dreams, and desires, then we don't have to be afraid of Him taking those things away or withholding them from us.

The desire for marriage came from Him in the first place, so I can rest assured that as I walk with Him, one of two things will happen:

1. He will fulfill that desire in His perfect timing, or...

2. He will slowly and gently change my desire. As long as I'm walking *with Him,* then I don't have to be afraid of that happening, because I trust my Father to lead me only in good ways!

So let us no longer wrestle with the question of whether or not marriage is "to be or not to be." Let us no longer wonder if our desires for human companionship are immovable obstacles between God and us.

God has given us a desire for covenant. We must simply realize that the relationship between God and Adam was established first, and *then* came marriage – man and wife. The two relationships were never intended to compete with one another, but to coexist in a perfect display of both natural and supernatural love.

If you are still concerned about it, ask God. Ask Him, if He wants you to remain single, to remove the desire to be married. And ask Him, if He wants you to marry, to help you keep that desire secondary to your love and relationship with Him.

Trust Him with your desires and your emotions. He is faithful to take care of everything we entrust to Him!

The Lord will perfect that which concerns me...
Psalm 138:8 NKJV

Chapter Eight
IS THERE SUCH THING AS THE ONE?

Our vocabulary as Christian singles often includes verbiage like, *"the one* God has for me" or "waiting for *the one."* However, I know that many of us probably wonder, "Is there really such thing as *the one* God has for me?"

This can be a touchy subject. On one hand, the hopeful romantic in us wants to believe that absolutely yes, there is that perfect someone out there just for us – the one who fits us and whom we fit, the one we click with in spite of all our quirks and flaws. On the other hand, the cautious realist in us doubts the likelihood of finding that one person in a sea of seven billion people in the world, so maybe it's best just to look for someone compatible with our personality, life goals, and belief system. From a spiritual perspective, we tend to believe God has a plan for each of us, but we also know He has given us free will to make our own choices. So the answer to our question is not crystal clear, to say the least.

What does God say? Could it be true that God really has *one* particular person in mind for me? If we're going to broach the subject, then we have to be aware of the kinds of questions it raises. If there is such thing as *the one,* then, "What if one of us misses God's plan for our lives, and we never meet?" "What if I already had a failed marriage that I thought was *the one*? Did I miss my chance, or will the next one be *the one?"*

When it comes to matters of God's plan and human will, theologians have spent countless hours debating how the two interact with one another. I don't want to get bogged down in detailed theological discussions here; I just want to offer us some biblical perspective to help each of us settle this issue in our own hearts. I will share with you how I look at this subject and why, but I think we'd do ourselves a favor by admitting right now that there's no concrete answer, so it's okay if we see this differently. Each of us needs to trust God to guide and shape our mindsets, so that individually we can walk in peace with Him. However, I do think we should lay a few foundational principles to build upon:

1. **Believing in *the one* does not absolve you of personal maturity and responsibility.** It seems that some people have the mindset that since God has *the one* picked out for them, they have no role to play in the matter, so they sit around, twiddling their proverbial thumbs while waiting for God to drop the relationship in their laps. We still have a role to play, at the very least, in developing our own personal maturity.

   To understand what I mean, let's play off of the car example from the first chapter. If a dad promises his 16-year-old son that he'll buy him a car one day, the son still has the responsibility of preparing himself for the gift to come. Becoming a safe, reliable driver is the best way he can prove to his dad that he's ready for that gift. Likewise, our devoting our attention to becoming mature, responsible individuals – people of integrity who love God and love other people – is the best way we can show our Father God that we're ready for the gift to come.

2. **We don't have to play into the culture's dating scene to make it happen.** Continuing the analogy, notice that I didn't say the teenager needs to go test-drive every model of car on the market to get himself ready for the dad's gift. Test driving does nothing to prepare him to be a good driver. Test drives are all about bells and whistles, high emotions, and cheap thrills. We take the car out, use it as a temporary feel-good, then turn it back into the dealer.

Unfortunately, our current dating scene is way too much like this. We have a lot of people out there test-driving other people. I'm sure you know exactly what I mean. Dating relationships in our culture tend to be based on the bells and whistles, and they last as long as the thrill is there; once their usefulness for making us feel good is over, we trade in that relationship for another one to try out.

We singles tend to bounce between these two extremes. Either we think that God has it all figured out, so we don't have to do anything, or we think that we need to jump in and "test-drive" a bunch of relationships to try to find what we like best – in other words, to help God make it happen. I believe both extremes are unhealthy and unbalanced.

3. **Believing in *the one* doesn't mean everything will be easy.** Regardless of where you land on the question of *the one,* I urge you to remember what we discussed in our chapter about True Love. Love is a decision. Even if God brings *the one* to you and smacks both of you in the

face or writes a message on a wall to let you know this is *the one*, your love for one another will still be based on a daily decision to each other. Believing in *the one* doesn't eliminate the mundane routine that so many couples get bored in; it doesn't free us from temptation's attempts to invade our lives; and it doesn't make everything easy. While we're busy being romantic about believing God has *the one* He has chosen for us, let's also be realistic that once we're paired together, we will still have to roll up our sleeves and put work into the relationship, just like any successful couple does. Love is a daily decision.

WHAT IS *THE ONE*?

Christians seem to look at this term in different ways. For some, *the one* is the belief that God has chosen a specific man for a specific woman. For others, *the one* is a belief that God will honor our decisions, and that as we walk with Him, He will cause our marriage – to whomever that may be – to become *the one* for us. While I have always leaned more toward the first definition, I really don't have a problem with the second one, either.

Personally, I tend to believe that for those of us who will get married one day, God has someone specific in mind for each of us to marry. However, I also believe strongly in the power of a decision, in which God blesses the decisions we make as long as they line up with His Word. While some may disagree, I think it is possible to believe in *the one* in both of these contexts simultaneously. Let's look at both sides so I can show you what I mean.

THE ONE: A SPECIFIC MAN FOR A SPECIFIC WOMAN

Again, this is my personal viewpoint: I believe God created me for one particular man, and I believe He created that man for me. Why do I believe that?

First of all, I just can't imagine that this loving Father we have, who holds so many good things for us, would leave something as hugely important as our lifelong spouses up to mere chance. And I certainly hope He doesn't leave it entirely up to me, because I've proven to be a pretty lousy judge of character when under the influence of emotional attraction to guys! I'll reiterate that that doesn't mean I have no responsibility on my end; I'm just expressing my hope that God will help direct me in a matter as important as this one. I don't want to be left to figure it all out by myself! I need His guidance, no matter what.

Second, while there's no Bible verse that defines *the one* in exactly these words, by looking at what is modeled for us in Scripture, it is hard for me to conclude otherwise. I'll show you what I mean.

The Greatest Romance Story

Once again, I go back to the beginning, giving heavy consideration to what God did when He first created humanity and when He first created marriage. Why do I do that? I guess it intrigues me to discover God's initial plan, study His original design, and evaluate that small slice of time when everything was pure and untainted, exactly as He wanted it before sin and human will started messing with things.

For a brief moment in time in the Garden, romance existed between two people without the presence of sin. Marriage existed without strife, lust, or competition. In a way, Adam and Eve shared the greatest romance story ever. They're the only two people who have ever experienced a perfect marriage, even if only for a short time before their disobedience allowed sin to infiltrate the human race. So considering just the perfect part, what do I see in their story?

Here's what I see: God created Eve from Adam, for Adam. We already looked in-depth at how God gave Adam the need for a companion. It is clear that Eve was the answer to the need God gave Adam. She was *the one* for him.

> *And the Lord God caused a deep sleep to fall on Adam, and he slept; and He took one of his ribs, and closed up the flesh in its place. Then the rib which the Lord God had taken from man He made into a woman, and He brought her to the man* (Genesis 2:21 – 22 NKJV).

Sometimes, to more clearly identify what we do see, I like to think about what we don't see. We don't see God creating five or ten women and parading them in front of Adam for him to choose his wife. We don't see God creating a big group of men and women and sending them off to run around the Garden, date each other for a while, and then pair up to marry whomever they are attracted to most.

Instead, we see that God very intentionally formed one, specific woman to be Adam's wife, and then He brought them together. The moment strikes me quite opposite from the way our dating culture treats relationships today, flippantly and erratically, full of trial and error (lots of trials and lots of errors). This moment when God brings Eve to Adam strikes me as full of awe, with reverence lingering in the air as Adam sees Eve for the first time. His words reveal his awareness that this woman standing in front of him completes him in a divinely destined way:

> *This is now bone of my bones and flesh of my flesh; She shall be called Woman, because she was taken out of Man* (Genesis 2:23 NKJV).

Adam and Eve's example stands out to me most, because theirs was the story God crafted without the competing influence of sin in their hearts. However, you may argue, *Yeah, but they were the only two people on earth; it was easy for them to find each other. How does this apply to us today?* Again, you'll have to come to your own conclusions, but I see it this way: It was still God who brought them together, who crafted their moment. "Then the Lord God... brought her to the man" (Genesis 2:22). Sure, in today's world, we have tons of people vying for our attention, but that's all the more reason that we need to keep our eyes on God and trust Him to direct our steps. Don't you think if He is big enough to perform open-abdomen surgery and form an entire woman from Adam's rib in order to orchestrate their meeting, He is also big enough to orchestrate the meeting when He brings each of us to *the one* He has for us?

If you're still unsure, that's okay. Thankfully, the earth's human population didn't stay at "two" for very long. Let's look in the Bible at a few couples whose marriages seem to have been brought together specifically and purposely by God Himself.

Models of Marriage

Isaac and Rebekah. We talked earlier about how Abraham sent his servant to find a wife for Isaac. Even though I'm thankful I won't be the subject of a marriage arranged by my parents (or their employees), something still strikes me as special about this story; there's a divine thread that runs through it. We see that Abraham assured the servant, "The Lord... will send his angel with you and make your journey a success, so that you can get a wife for my son..." (Genesis 24:40). When he arrived at his destination, the servant prayed and asked for God's specific guidance to help him recognize *the one*:

> Then he prayed, "Lord, God of my master Abraham, make me successful today... May it be that when I say to a young woman, 'Please let down your jar that I may have a drink,' and she says, 'Drink, and I'll water your camels too' – let her be **the one** you have chosen for your servant Isaac..." (Genesis 24:12 – 14 NKJV).

I don't know about you, but I find the story incredibly romantic. The servant didn't pray for God to show him a woman who would be compatible with Isaac. He prayed that God would show him "the one you have chosen for your servant Isaac." Let's zoom in on several key points in this one phrase. First, he actually prayed for "the one" to be revealed. Second, the words, "you have chosen," indicate that *the one* had been chosen by God before the servant arrived. Third, he specified, "for your servant Isaac," revealing that God's choice was person-specific. This servant clearly believed that God had one particular woman whom He had chosen to be the wife for

Isaac. Therefore, the servant was only interested in finding *the one.*

If you read on, you'll see that before the servant had even finished praying, God led Rebekah to him and confirmed to him that she was *the one,* exactly as he has prayed. We looked earlier at the moment Isaac and Rebekah met – another moment filled with awe and reverence, when two people realized that God had brought them together.

Boaz and Ruth. There is a beautiful hope to be found in this story, not only for those of us seeking *the one,* but also for anyone reading this who once was married but is now single again. We see an example of a God-ordained *second* marriage when we consider Ruth and Boaz. In this case, Ruth is a young widow; after her husband's death, she has now returned with her mother-in-law, also widowed, to a land completely foreign to Ruth. Here she is, single again through no fault of her own, left to fend for herself; instead of taking the easy route, she has decided to stick by her mother-in-law and do her best to provide for both of them. Ruth is marked by her unselfish, immovable loyalty and by her hard work ethic, both of which the wealthy and noble Boaz notices immediately (Ruth 2:5 – 12). This prominent, generous businessman takes her as his wife, not only providing Ruth a sheltering, protective love, but also ensuring her mother-in-law is cared for (Ruth 3:17, 4:9). What a catch, huh? I mean, it's an awesome thing for a man to be considerate of his wife's mother, but how many men would take care of their wife's *first husband's* mother? Boaz was Ruth's knight in shining armor, so to speak, her happily ever after.

While God blessed their marriage in and of itself, Boaz and Ruth's marriage was not only for their sakes; God had purposes for their union that were bigger than they were. Do you recall the shepherd-boy-turned-giant-killer who wrote many of the Psalms and also became the king of Israel – David? He was Boaz and Ruth's great-grandson. By marrying Boaz, Ruth not only became an ancestor to David, one of the most beloved characters in the Bible, but she also was inserted into the ancestry line of Jesus Christ (see Matthew 1). What a beautiful outcome for a woman who had seen such hardship early on in life! God never stopped looking out for her; He led her to *the one* after her first one, and He even wrote them together into the pages of history.

Joseph and Mary. Let's look at just one more for now. Consider Joseph and Mary, the mother of Jesus. We often give most of our attention to Mary, but the Bible also clearly traces Jesus' ancestry through His earthly father, Joseph (Matthew 1). Not just any woman could have been Joseph's fiancée, the pure young woman whom God entrusted to give birth to His Son. Likewise, not just any man could have been the husband-to-be to a pregnant virgin. I know we tend to give Mary the credit for Jesus' birth (after all, she said "yes" to the angel's prophecy when she could have said "no," and it was her body that went through the pregnancy and delivery; that's pretty significant). However, we sometimes overlook how instrumental Joseph was in the process. See, Joseph also had to say "yes" to the angel's instruction (Matthew 1:18 – 24). And Joseph, as the husband and father, is the one the angel warned when Baby Jesus' life was in danger; Joseph took his family and led them to safety. It was Joseph again who received the angel's message when it was safe to return to Israel (Matthew 2:13 - 23).

Bringing Jesus into the world and raising the Son of God was a big deal, and it required two people hand-chosen by God for the task. It was no accident that God brought this man and this woman together; He specifically wanted them together to carry out His purposes in a big way.

Nothing Less than God's Best

When we see examples of God's using divinely connected husband-and-wife duos so powerfully for His kingdom, how can we help but want the same for ourselves? These couples inspire me in my faith that God indeed has specific, custom-crafted plans for each of our lives. History would look much different if these marriages had never taken place the way they did. God powerfully uses men and women joined together in marriage covenant by Him. With that in mind, I don't want to settle for just "okay." I believe God has greater plans in store for my future marriage, and I believe He has the same for you, too!

With that said, let me explain how I see the other side of believing in *the one* as well.

THE ONE: THE POWER OF A DECISION

There seems to be a push in today's church culture to remind Christians of our responsibility as human beings to make decisions, to stop using "waiting on God" as a cop-out for doing nothing. On one hand, I fully understand where this is coming from. As a pastor's kid, I've witnessed far too many people who lived paralyzed by indecision while they sought God for answers, then made poor decisions and blamed it on God's voice. On the other hand, God still speaks to us today by Holy Spirit's living in us, and He will prompt and lead us in the decisions we should make (Isaiah 30:21; Proverbs 3:6; John 14:16 – 17).

I believe in being so close to the Holy Spirit that if He wants to direct me in something, even if it is seemingly insignificant, I am open to hearing and obeying His direction. I also believe in taking personal responsibility as a mature Christian to be able to make decisions for myself that will line up with the Word of God. When I am cultivating my relationship with God, I should be growing not only as an individual but also in my understanding of His Truth and His heart. There are some things He won't have to speak to me about directly, because I can know the answers simply by knowing His Word.

When I was growing up, there were some things that my parents had to tell us kids over and over until we remembered on our own. We used to laugh, because every time we would sit down to eat, my little sister would have to go to the restroom. My parents would excuse her to go, she would run down the hall, then a few minutes later, she would come running back toward the kitchen. One of my parents would ask, "Did you wash your hands?" She would stop in her tracks with wide eyes, do an about-face, and run back down the hall. In those days, they had to remind her constantly to wash her hands after going to the restroom. Guess what? Now that she's an adult, no one has to tell her to wash her hands! She eventually remembered on her own.

Here's another example. When I was a teenager, I never had to ask my mom if she wanted me to clean my room. My mother loves to have her house neat, organized, and clean. By growing up in our home, I knew not to leave clothes lying around on the floor, not to leave dirty dishes on the table, and not to move the condiments from the door of the refrigerator to the shelf (condiments did not belong on the regular shelves in our refrigerator). There are some things that you might not have known if you were a houseguest with us for a week, but I know them simply from living all those years with my mom. I know her preferences, her expectations, and overall, her heart. Once I got old enough to know these things, she didn't have to tell them to me anymore. I just knew them, and I acted accordingly.

We need to understand that, if there are seasons of life when we seem to draw closer to God and really push to learn how to hear His voice, we will gain a closeness in those seasons that will help us learn His preferences, His expectations, and His heart. Then there will be times that we are faced with a decision and won't necessarily have to stop, kneel down, and pray about what to do. Some things will be clear to us because of the maturity and intimacy we have already gained by getting to know Him. Romans 12:2 shows us how we can discover God's will simply by walking with Him, allowing Him to shape our character:

> *Don't copy the behavior and customs of this world, but let God transform you into a new person by changing the way you think. Then you will learn to know God's will for you, which is good and pleasing and perfect* (Romans 12:2 NLT).

Relating this to the issue of *the one,* this is why I don't necessarily have a problem with it if not every Christian couple feels that they specifically heard God's voice telling them this is *the one.* The main thing is that our hearts should be in a constant position of submission to the Holy Spirit, so He *can* guide us in any and every way. And yes, there will be times that we do seek Him for a specific answer. In either case, remember the promise in Proverbs 3:6, "In all your ways acknowledge Him, and He shall direct your paths" (NKJV). The security of knowing He is guiding your decisions comes from acknowledging Him in all our ways. We run into trouble when we refuse to acknowledge Him, shutting Him out of the decision because of fear that He will say "no" to something we think we want.

James 1:5 says, "If any of you lacks wisdom, let him ask God, who gives generously to all without reproach, and it will be given him" (ESV). Sometimes God gives us a specific answer when we're seeking guidance in a decision, but many times He calls us to act on wisdom – simply put, a spiritual-meets-natural level of common sense. This wisdom will guide us into making decisions that the Lord can bless! God can bless decisions that line up with His Word.

So in this regard, if we're following His voice and following His wisdom, then yes, I do believe we can choose a spouse and ask God to bless our union. While I personally am convinced that God will give me His help in finding *the one* He has for me specifically, I also contend that we need to be mature Christians, seeking Him first and trusting Him to direct our every step.

Compatible Companions

I know what some of you are thinking. The concept of *the one* is great for those of us who are seeking God, trusting Him, and waiting for Him to bring us together with our future spouses. But a lot of people enter into marriage under other circumstances, perhaps before they knew Christ. In other words, a lot of marriages began without either spouse seeking God beforehand about it. So when it comes to this subject of *the one* ordained by God, is all hope lost for them to live out this same dream?

My answer to that question is no, hope is not lost. Again, I believe in the power of decision, and if two people make the decision to stay committed to one another in marriage covenant, regardless of how the relationship started before they knew Christ, then God absolutely can cause their marriage to become all they could hope for and more. (To clarify further, a couple should never divorce over the realization that they didn't seek God before getting married! Once married, the entire conversation changes; instead of looking for a way out, the couple should look for God's help in making the relationship work).

Ultimately, here is where I stand on questions like this: **We should never underestimate God's Grace, nor should we underestimate His ability to work through people even when we aren't aware of it.** Let me give you an example of what I mean, an example that is very close to my heart:

> I have been blessed with two incredible sets of grandparents; all four individuals have been shining

examples throughout my life of what it means to love God, follow Him wholeheartedly, and give of oneself unselfishly to help others. All four grandparents were actively involved in ministry for longer than I've been alive. They set in motion a wonderful legacy for our family, a legacy of God's love and faithfulness. Not only did they model selfless devotion to God, but they also modeled what successful marriages look like. My dad's parents were married for 52 years before my grandfather passed away, and my mom's parents were married for 62 years before my grandmother passed away just recently. Both couples are heroes in my book, personifying what *"til death do us part"* looks like. However, these two couples got started in marriage very differently from one another.

My mom's parents came together as a result of my grandmother's having been raised in a preacher's home, the same preacher who helped mentor a sincere young man just starting out in ministry. Ministry brought these two together when they were teenagers, and they never looked back. Their 62 years of marriage reflected just as many years of ministry and loving the Lord together.

My dad's parents met and married under drastically different circumstances. My grandfather was a World War Two combat veteran, a rugged Navy sailor who saw the violence of D-Day firsthand when his ship arrived at Utah Beach. My grandmother was an only child from a single parent home (which was much rarer in the 1930s than it is today); her father had deserted her and her mother to run off with another woman. My grandmother had learned to look out for herself; she was independent, no-nonsense, and perhaps even a tad feisty, based on the stories she told me. The tough Navy soldier met the small-town girl from a broken home, and there wasn't much consideration of God's will when they got married. In fact, it wasn't until several years later, after they were already raising their four sons, when both my grandfather and my grandmother gave their lives to Jesus. That decision changed their lives, and the rest, as they say, is history.

I don't know how God did it, but I believe with all my heart that He brought my dad's parents together, even in spite of their own unawareness at the time. Some may argue that He didn't bring them together, but once they gave their lives to Him, He worked everything out for their good. If you see it that way, I don't have a problem with that. Whether they were created for one another by God Himself or they were simply two highly compatible companions whose union He blessed, they were two peas in a pod. From my own perspective, I don't doubt that my grandfather was *the one* for my granny and vice versa. Besides, if they had never come together, I wouldn't be here right now! Our family story would have ended up much differently. As it is, God fabricated a beautiful legacy out their marriage. And either way, the success of their marriage required both the Grace of God as well as the element of their own decision.

Ultimately, whatever the circumstances, I believe God's Love and Grace are bigger than we are. For those who fear they missed *the one,* let's just consider a few key points:

1. In all things...

> *And we know that **in all things** God works for the good of those who love him, who have been called according to his purpose"* (Romans 8:28).

He doesn't apply this only to those who grew up knowing Christ or to those who always walked His paths. He applies it to those who love Him and have been called according to His purpose. So no matter what situations you face today as a result of past circumstances, I still believe God can work *all things* together for your good!

2. **Nothing catches God by surprise.** God isn't scrambling to catch up with your mistakes. While He gave you free will to make your own decisions, you didn't shock Him with what those decisions were. Psalm 33 says this:

> *The Lord looks down from heaven and sees the whole human race. From his throne he observes all who live on the earth. He made their hearts, so he understands everything they do* (Psalm 33:13 – 15 NLT).

I love movies in which we as the audience think the good guy's mission has been totally thwarted, only to find out in the end that the hero's original plan was never thrown off-track by the various obstacles that surfaced along the way. I see God that way. I believe He's always got an ace up His sleeve, so to speak, in order to bring you back to the center of His plan at any point that you surrender to Him.

3. **God can turn any situation around.** Remember, He turned some blue-collar fishermen into world evangelists; He turned a shepherd boy into a mighty king; and He turned a murdering persecutor of Christians into one of the most passionate forces ever to spread the Gospel. No one is outside of His reach. Furthermore, He sees far more potential in people than we could possibly begin to see ourselves.

Every marriage is made up of two people full of such potential. But each of these two people also has a free will. If one individual chooses to walk in sin and rebellion, I believe God's network of Grace is so incredibly vast and intertwined through all of us that He can still create good for the spouse who is submitted to Him. We can never begin to understand how He does things. He just does them, and He calls what He creates, "good."

TRUSTING GOD'S PLAN

We're going to talk more about God's Grace for our bad choices later on. For now, let's wrap up the discussion on *the one* with some thoughts about God's plan for our lives.

If you find your mind whirling with unanswered questions, try to take comfort in the fact that it's okay not to understand everything. After all, our Father Himself tells us:

As the heavens are higher than the earth, so are my ways higher than your ways and my thoughts than your thoughts (Isaiah 55:9).

I don't take His words here as condescending toward us. On the contrary, I imagine a loving, patient parent telling his child after much inquisition, "You'll understand this when you get a little older; for now, just trust Daddy that what I'm saying is true." Don't stress if not all of your questions are answered. Remember, we can still live in God's Peace Express – that peace that passes our understanding. And we can still walk in His beautiful, masterful plan for us!

So whether you believe in *the one* or not, let's be sure our faith and confidence rest solely in *The One* who loves us above all others; God our Father will take care of us and lead us as we acknowledge Him in all our ways!

Who are those who fear the Lord?
He will show them the path they should choose.
Psalm 25:12 NLT

Chapter Nine
PROMISES & PURPOSE, DREAMS & DESTINY

I love to think and talk about the plans God has for us. We know that God does have a plan for each of us, even though we often don't understand the full realm of His purposes as thoroughly as we'd like! God's ways are beyond what we can really imagine. Just consider the vastness of His plan in light of Psalm 139:16:

> *You saw me before I was born. Every day of my life was recorded in your book. Every moment was laid out before a single day had passed* (NLT).

I've had a keen awareness for most of my life that my destiny is intertwined with the man God has for me, whoever and wherever he may be. On one hand, a realization like that is exciting! On the other hand, it can be overwhelming, making us feel even more pressure to do everything right so we can find *the one*. It can even be paralyzing when we become afraid to pursue our own destiny in fear that we will choose a path that leads us away from *the one*.

I invite you to join me in temporarily pushing "pause" in your mind about whatever your future husband's destiny is. If we can keep our eyes on our Father, trusting Him to lead us in His path for us now, He will undoubtedly arrange those divine meetings for each of us when it comes time to introduce us to *the one*.

PATHWAYS VERSUS MOMENTS

The Lord says,
"I will guide you along the best pathway for your life.
I will advise you and watch over you."
Psalm 32:8 NLT

As a very goal-oriented person, I have had the tendency to section off my life by landmarks and accomplishments (such as graduation from high school, then college; getting my first real job; getting my first raise; eventually, getting married). I would reach one goal and immediately set my sights on the next one. Of course, in and of itself, that's not a bad thing; it's a pretty good way to be productive. However, I had to break free from the idea that my destiny was merely a moment in time waiting to happen. Otherwise, I would waste the day I'm given today, because my eyes would be set on a day somewhere out in my future. Furthermore, if I didn't have "the next big thing," another big goal lined up to strive toward, I could quickly go from being driven to being apathetic, having a hard time finding the purpose in each ordinary day.

One of the most liberating truths I have learned about the purpose God has for each of us is this: **Destiny is not a destination; it is a journey.** As the Psalm above says, God leads us "along the best *pathway*." We tend to zero in on moments along the way, and we're afraid of missing our moment. However, if we can trust God to lead us on the best pathway, then that includes every moment along the way.

See, if we live for just one event or even just one season of life, whether it be a moment of recognition on a platform, a successful entrepreneurial endeavor, or even a wedding day, we reduce the value we place on our lives to a mere fraction of what God originally intended for us. Furthermore, we take today for granted. God has packed each day of our lives full of potential and purpose. I wonder how many "todays" we have wasted by looking so far out into the future that we couldn't clearly see the opportunities in front of us right now. We have to come to the place, whether single or married, dating or not dating, where we recognize that destiny is not simply the fulfillment of one of our dreams. Destiny is the road – the pathway – that keeps us aligned with the purpose and plans God has for our lives.

Sometimes we strive so hard to discover our destiny that we become disheartened and confused, and it's tempting just to give up, to resort to a "c'est la vie" or "such is life" outlook. Destiny can be an overwhelming concept unless we break it down and realize that each day is an opportunity to walk out the plans God has for that day. More than that, we must realize that God doesn't plop us on Earth blindfolded and leave us to figure everything out by ourselves! He doesn't leave us on Destiny Road alone or unequipped. In addition to the guidance in His Word, He gives us three beautifully divine signposts along our pathway to help us: promises, dreams, and passions.

SIGN 1: PROMISES

These are the givens, the things that God guarantees on His end, although they are oftentimes conditional on how we handle our end. Promises are things like, "Honor your father and mother, so that you may live long..." (Exodus 20:12). The Bible is packed full of promises God has already given us. It is utterly astounding to take some time and look at all wonderful blessings God has stored up for us, His children. When we bow out of our own pity parties, stop moaning and whining about how unfulfilled we are without a husband, and start focusing on the phenomenal promises God has given us, we will find ourselves maturing at an accelerated pace.

Fixing our attention on God's promises will also help us gain a greater understanding of who we really are, reminding us that we are chosen by God, we are royalty in His eyes, and we are holy and special to Him (1 Peter 2:9). I urge you to stop evaluating yourself by how many heads you turn as you walk through the mall today, by how many nice compliments or even seductive comments you receive at work this week, or by how many men have or haven't asked you out this year. This may sound harsh, but it's time to get over yourself! Whether you have too much pride or too little self-esteem, remember that your value comes back to how God sees you; His promises to you are a huge indicator of how highly He thinks of you. It's time to lift your head from the horizontal affirmation you're used to seeking from men, and instead start seeking out God's *promises* for you, His Word over you.

God's promises help assure us that we are on the right pathway, that we are right in the middle of Destiny Road.

SIGN 2: DREAMS

Dreams are a great indicator of destiny. A lot can be told about a person by knowing what she aspires to, by understanding her dreams – or lack thereof.

Our dreams expose a lot about the position of our hearts. Are our dreams self-centered, or do they seek the good of other people? Do we have dreams of making something of ourselves to prove to everyone else that we could, or do we dream of helping others make something of themselves? Do we dream of becoming noble women of integrity and character, or do we dream of all the attention we could gain by being more attractive and sexy, irresistible to men everywhere?

Unfortunately, from experience, I know where many of our dreams start and stop: We dream of finally snagging the husband we've been waiting so long for. We don't really see beyond that. That is Mission Number One. It's the only thing on our radar.

This may be difficult for us to swallow, but in order to live in the fullness of abundant life, our vision has to reach beyond the sole dream for a lifelong partner. As badly and as long as we may have desired our spouses, if finding our husbands is our only dream, the only motivation and inspiration of our hearts, then we are living and dreaming far below God's potential for our lives. We will miss out on some of the greatest blessings God has for us unless we allow Him to change our focus.

Stifled Potential, Silenced Dreams

Have you ever seen a woman whose potential you knew was being stifled because of the man she was with? I'm sure we all have. We've all seen those codependent relationships, the ones where we want to grab the person we love, shake them by the shoulders, and say, *Can't you see you deserve better?! Can't you see this relationship is a dead-end road?!* But in many cases, she can't see the Truth, because she's too wrapped up in the controlling, manipulative nature of the relationship. She can't see Truth, because she stopped dreaming long ago; what was in front of her drowned out her dreams.

When you confine your heart and vision to dreaming only of having a mate and nothing else, you are essentially slipping blinders over your eyes, allowing yourself to fall victim to the same controlling spirit that wants to cripple your potential and destiny. When you have only this one dream, you set yourself up for failure and hardship, because nothing else matters to you as much as ending the season of Single. So consider this chapter my taking you by the shoulders – out of sisterly love, of course, – shaking you, and saying, *Can't you see you deserve more? Can't you see our Father has so many good things lined up for you?*

Dream More, Fear Less

Your life holds so much potential, both now and in the future. Your heart holds so many dreams that you have yet to discover. What is keeping you from dreaming those dreams? I know one answer: Fear.

It's crazy how our minds play games with us. If you're like me, you know what it is to long for that perfect companion so badly that you're afraid that if you dream too many dreams, you will limit the pool of possible men too greatly and may never find someone to fit. Maybe I'm the odd one out here, but have you ever thought things like:

> ➤ *I would love to have my own business one day, but what if I marry a man who wants me to be a full-time homemaker?*

> ➤ *I would love to travel and perform, but what if I get married and don't want to be apart from my husband too much?*

> ➤ *I would love to get into public speaking, but what if my future husband doesn't want an outspoken wife?*

Again, maybe I'm the only one and no one else has ever thought like that. But in case you can relate, let me share what I've come to realize.

This kind of mindset stalls us on our path of destiny. We can't put our lives on hold, limiting all of our other dreams based solely on what may or may not happen in terms of this one dream. Besides, if God knows the desires of our hearts (and put them there in the first place), don't you think He will match us with the husbands whose dreams, desires, and personalities will be a perfect complement to ours, and vice versa?

How presumptuous we have been to think that God's destiny for our lives has not yet begun!

So many of us are sitting around nervously twiddling our thumbs or primping our hair while we wait for Prince Charming; meanwhile, we're missing out on worlds of destiny God has for us right now!

Expand Your Horizons

If the main dream of your life is finding and being with that special someone, you are inhibiting your own destiny in three ways:

1. **You are giving yourself tunnel vision.** However unintentionally, you are allowing yourself to become a self-centered person, because you have only this one goal in life. You cannot see the needs of others around you - at least not in the capacity that you could - and if you do notice the outside world, you see it only through the tainted glass of, "I'm single, and I've got to get un-single as soon as possible."

2. **You are setting yourself up for being unfulfilled.** Ok, so let's say you round the corner at the grocery store this evening and run right into Mr. God's-Best-for-You. The next six months to a year play out as the perfect romance you always dreamed of, and before you know it, you are Mrs. God's-Best-for-You, happily married to this wonderful gift from God. Ok, so now what? Oh wait. You didn't dream anything beyond finding this man sitting on the couch next to you, so now that you've reached this point of the journey, you have absolutely no vision beyond this moment.

The problem with fairy tales is that they spend all their time describing the events that lead up to Happily Ever After. No one ever talks about what Happily Ever After looks like. Unfortunately, many of us dream for our futures in the same way. We dream up to that one moment, but after that, we have no idea, either, because we never took time to think about it. Our tunnel vision was only focused on this one thing. Now we have it, so what's next?

3. **You are setting yourself up for compromise.** If your main focus is to be un-alone, you will begin forfeiting the dreams God wants you to dream for your mate in order to have a right-now companion.

God actually has ideas and desires and dreams He wants to give you, even about your future spouse, but you can get so busy searching that you won't find time to cultivate those dreams. Instead of measuring a potential mate against God's standards and the dreams He has for you, you will spend your time trying to make any guy be *the* guy. Just remember, **most of the men in your social circles *won't* meet the criteria of God's Best for you.** So please, for your sake and theirs, stop trying to make them. Be willing to take a pass and wait for God to bring the one to you who fits His dreams for you perfectly. I can tell you from experience that compromising and trying to settle for less is just not worth it.

I shared with you earlier about the seven-month relationship I was in with Mr. Not-Right-for-Me. I was trying to fit "a guy" into the "the guy" slot in my life. I knew he didn't fit the dreams I held dear in my heart, but I was willing to trade a lifetime of dreams in order to try to fill the sole dream of getting married; that seemed to be the most important thing. I realized later that while I'm sure this guy matched someone else's dreams, he didn't match mine.

I don't know who said it originally, but it is so true: **The only thing harder than waiting for God is wishing you had.**

Over the last few years since that relationship ended, God has awakened in me the desire to dream again. Although I tried to settle for "a guy," God had many more dreams He wanted to dream through me. Now that I have begun dreaming again, I not only dream about my husband, but I've also expanded my horizons. I am dreaming of the direction my ministry is taking, what good I can do for God's kingdom. I am dreaming of having this manuscript published to help other women discover joy in the journey of Single. I am dreaming of business and financial endeavors. I am dreaming of a godly marriage and the wonderful children we will have one day.

Now, will reality confront my dreams at some point? Might these dreams turn out differently than I think right now? Absolutely. But reality is never a valid reason to refuse to dream altogether. I entrust my dreams to my Father. He can mold and shape and tweak and change them as He sees fit. It's just so much fun to be able to dream again! I've decided to enjoy the journey regardless of what each specific outcome will look like. As a side note, I am finding that the more I dream in other areas in life, the more liberated I am to dream of my husband without obsessing like I used to do. God is so great! He doesn't withhold anything good from His kids, but He will delay giving it to us until He knows it will be freedom to us instead of bondage!

Dreams, coupled with God's promises, are a powerful catalyst on the road of Destiny. Before we move on, however, let's consider the third sign God gives us along the way, to help keep us positioned just right.

SIGN 3: PASSION

That's a loaded word. On one hand, it is exciting to be passionate about something or someone; on the other hand, we often link the idea of passion with fleshly, negative, or even sinful desires. Passion is basically an outward expression of inward emotion, and emotions can be very powerful in either a good way or a very negative way.

Did you know that passion can actually be a tool to help keep you on your path of destiny? Here's the key: **Do not let your perspective become tainted by mere emotion.** Passion must be tempered with perspective.

What do I mean by that? Your passion and your perspective are co-dependent on each other. Your perspective – the way you see things – is the foundation that your passion is built upon. However, if your passions – your strong feelings and driving force – become distorted or even perverted, so does your perspective. As one moves, so does the other.

This is why it is so important for us to keep our minds submitted to God's will, focused on His Word and His best for our lives. This is why it is imperative that we have the mind of Christ and why it is so very, very important for us to guard our hearts, the seat of our emotions. Our emotions really do influence everything else in our lives.

Think about this for a minute: Do we ever really have a bad mood? If I look honestly at the days that I felt I was in a bad mood, the truth is that I can trace the "mood" back to one or two things that triggered a negative emotion in me, and that emotion influenced and took over everything else in my life that day. I called it a "bad mood," when in reality, it was simply an emotion allowed to go unchecked. I failed to rein it in, guard my heart, and maintain the perspective I know as Truth, so by default, the emotion ruled my day and skewed my perspective. I may have thought people were being rude to me who weren't; I may have thought my boss was unhappy about my work when he wasn't. My perspective shifted and labeled my mood and maybe even my day as "bad." What if I instead had taken authority over my emotions – because they are mine to control – and held true to the perspective of faith? I could have easily snuffed out that bad mood and changed the course of my day.

We have bought into the notion that passion – whether in the form an unchecked mood, a spontaneous rant to a co-worker, or even a sexual compulsion – is an unrestrained, uncontrollable force in our lives, but that's just not true. Many people have used unchecked passions as an excuse for doing whatever their flesh pleased instead of living in line with God's Word. From using a bad mood as an excuse to treat people rudely to using "God wants me to be happy" as an excuse to live in sexual sin, following out-of-control passions is a dangerous thing.

On the flip side, passions submitted to God are a beautiful thing. Yes, it may mean you have to do opposite of what "feels" right in the moment. Yes, it may mean you have to make tough decisions and discipline your fleshly nature to stay submitted to the Spirit. Yes, it may mean you have to smile and say a kind word when you're incredibly frustrated about something that happened this morning. But all of it is worth it when our lives begin to produce beauty instead of ugliness, self-control instead of no control, peace instead of conflict.

When we see these traits beginning to develop in our lives, we can take that as a sign that we are on the right track! See, walking with God – clinging to His promises and dreaming His dreams for our lives – will inevitably lead to His character being developed in us. How we handle our passions is one of the signs that indicate where we are in our growth and maturity in Him.

FOLLOWING THE SIGNS

Sometimes Destiny Road isn't as clear as we'd like it to be. There will be times that you may feel as if you're driving along a winding road in heavy fog; you can barely see two feet in front of you. I've driven in conditions like that many times on the interstate leading into Chattanooga, sometimes in heavy fog, sometimes in snow, sometimes at night; in all of these cases, visibility was severely limited. I had to rely on the guides, especially the white line on the right side of the road, to assure me that I wasn't going off-track and to help me know I was still on the pathway.

It's easy to drive on a dry road on a nice, clear day, when you can see for miles around. However, real life is going to bring foggy patches. All together, these three signposts God has given us – promises, dreams, and passion – will help reassure us that we're still on that beautiful road of God's destiny for our lives, even when visibility seems limited.

God's purposes for your life are full of promise and potential. Won't you join me in taking hold of our Father's hand and enjoying the journey?

Now to him who is able to do
immeasurably more than all we ask or imagine,
according to his power that is at work within us...
Ephesians 3:20

Chapter Ten

THE POWER OF PURITY, THE ESSENCE OF GRACE

Misunderstood. Underutilized. Unappreciated. Having so much to offer but being passed over for something that looks more exciting on the surface. If purity were a person, I imagine this is how she would feel today. Purity seems to be a foreign concept in our day and age. In our journey through Single, it is imperative that we understand purity and that we recognize all it has to offer us, regardless of what our experiences have been so far. Purity is not something to be taken for granted, no matter what your past or present looks like.

Maybe you're familiar with purity; maybe you've lived in purity rather successfully so far, or maybe you've failed miserably. Maybe you have no idea how to live in purity or gave up on the idea a long time ago. Perhaps your innocence was stripped away from you before you were old enough to know what was going on. Or maybe you once were part of the crowd that mocked purity, willingly giving away your sexuality as a rite of passage in your youth. No matter who you are or what your background, purity has a powerful role to play in your life if you will let it. In this chapter, I want to introduce you to purity in a new way. If you have regrets over the loss of your own innocence, then I also want to introduce you to a Grace that can cleanse you from the past and give you a new start. Will you join me? Together with all of our past experiences, mindsets, baggage, attempts, and failures – whatever we bring to the table – let's take a vulnerably open, fresh look at purity and learn about the power it offers us in our lives today.

PURITY AS A PROTECTOR

We've talked a lot about our Father's Love for us and how He loves to give His children good gifts. Purity is another one of those good gifts He has given us. However, contrary to what we may think, purity is not intended to be a burdensome restriction, nor is it supposed to be an ever-present guilt trip. Purity is more like a weapon that our loving Father has given us to protect ourselves physically, spiritually, mentally, and emotionally. I can see your eyebrows furrowing already. *A weapon? Really?*

For some of you, maybe a parent or someone close to you once gave you some kind of means of self-defense – pepper spray to keep on your keychain, a pocket knife, or even a handgun to carry in your purse. Maybe you don't carry a physical weapon, but perhaps an older brother or good friend taught you some basic self-defense maneuvers to help you escape if an attacker ever tried to subdue you. It's not something we generally like to think about, and while we may have varying opinions on the subject of weapons, I think we would at least agree that if a loved one has offered us this type of gift or instruction, they were doing so out of their love for us. They were motivated by their desire to help protect us, because they don't ever want us to fall victim to another person's violence or perversion.

Similarly, **purity is a gift our loving Father has given to help us protect ourselves against the enemy's attempts to strip us of our innocence.** The problem is that so many of us have the wrong idea of what purity is and how it is to be used.

See, we often think of purity as a physical state, such as virginity. The problem in thinking of purity that way is that we also think once that state has been compromised, our purity is lost forever. I want to show you how purity is so much more than that.

PURITY'S PATH

How can a young man keep his way pure?
By guarding it according to your word
Psalm 119:9 ESV

Purity is not a physical state. It is a lifestyle, a mindset, a series of protective choices. Notice the phrase in the verse above, "keep his *way* pure." Remember how we said destiny is a journey? Well, purity is also a path – a *way*. It's up to us to choose purity and to *guard* our way according to God's Word. Purity is not a one-time shot that, if you fail, is gone forever. Purity is a *way* of life, meant to be guarded consistently and vigilantly by living according to God's loving instructions for us in His Word, the Bible. Why is it so important to protect our path of purity?

When we protect our path, our path then protects us.

> *But you have upheld me because of my integrity, and set me in your presence forever* (Psalm 41:12 ESV).

Another version says it this way:

> *You have preserved my life because I am **innocent**; you have brought me into your presence forever* (NLT).

Our path of purity – of innocence and integrity – literally preserves our lives. Even if you feel your innocence and integrity have been destroyed, God is the restorer of all things. But we still have a role to play in actively guarding our paths from this point forward, and that role can start right now, today. Our path will then protect us physically, mentally, emotionally, and spiritually, because God wants to keep us safe in every way, not just one or two areas. Let me show you what I mean.

PARTIAL PURITY

I take issue with the way the church in general has taught sexual purity. It's not that I disagree with the fundamental goal, to help spur young people and single adults toward choosing abstinence. In fact, throughout my own adolescence and young adulthood, I was a huge supporter of the abstinence message, and I still am, since its foundation is in the Bible! However, I have come to realize that by parading the message of abstinence, we as the church have only been telling part of the story, and unfortunately, the part we're not telling is leaving many teens and single adults set up for failure.

The essence of the message we have been shouting has been, *Wait for sex! Abstinence is the way to purity! Abstinence is the ultimate victory; sex is the ultimate sin!* Again, I don't disagree with the desired outcome; I wish I could convince every teenager and single adult to walk in abstinence, because I know personally that it is worth it. I do, however, have a problem with the fact that, in trying to hammer a message into people's hearts and minds, we've left out much of the context needed to support the message. **We've been teaching partial purity, and partial purity isn't real purity at all.**

We must understand some key clarifications that often get left out of the conversation in our discussions of purity:

1. **If I can talk you into abstinence, someone else can talk you out of it.** If purity isn't established in your heart, your head will talk you out of it every time. It has to be deeper than a head-decision.

2. **When we equate abstinence to purity, we erroneously equate sex to impurity.** While both can be true in different settings, it is the setting that must be emphasized. In the setting of Single, sex is impure; however, in the setting of marriage, abstinence would be unhealthy! Remember, God created sex; the enemy perverted it. So let's make sure we aren't letting the notion that "sex is dirty" be implanted in our psyches.

3. **If abstinence equals purity, then married people don't have to worry about purity, right?** Wrong. If you've ever known a marriage ripped apart by infidelity or clouded by an addiction to pornography, then you know this couldn't be further from the truth. Purity is a lifelong pursuit that applies to people of every walk of life, male and female, single or married, young or old.

4. **If abstinence equals purity, then we automatically exclude from the conversation anyone who has already lost her virginity,** whether voluntarily or involuntarily. By hailing abstinence as the flagship component of our message, we have pushed away those

157

who perhaps needed the message most. I believe fully that, while we cannot undo the past, we can redefine our future, and we can be made pure again in the eyes of our Father. After all, it's His perception of us that really matters, anyway.

5. **MYTH: Abstinence leads to purity.**
TRUTH: Purity leads to abstinence (for those of us who are single, that is). Abstinence alone doesn't enable you to live in purity; it's only one component of the process. On the contrary, purity enables you to live in abstinence. **Abstinence alone is powerless to generate purity**, just as a light switch is powerless to create light by itself. The electricity must already be present, connecting the switch to the source of power, in order for the switch to facilitate light. Likewise, purity must already exist in the heart and mind, connecting us to the ultimate source of power – our Father – and then abstinence will be a vital component of that purity.

6. **Abstinence involves your body. Purity involves your whole being – spirit, soul, and body.** If abstinence by itself could generate purity, then why do you feel so dirty when you have a lustful thought? Why does your conscience prick you when you look at a pornographic image or watch a nude scene in a movie? You aren't actually *doing* anything physically, so why does it feel ... wrong? The reason is that purity begins in the heart, infiltrates the mind, and guides the body. Purity involves all of you.

This is where a minor adjustment can make a major difference. Purity can't be only skin-deep. We have to be willing to surrender impure thought habits, unhealthy viewing habits, our participation in crude conversation and vulgar jokes; we have to be willing to establish purity in every part of our lives. Ultimately, we have to allow our path of purity to be rooted in our relationship with our Father. *Would my Father enjoy listening to these lyrics with me? Would God laugh and chime in with this conversation? Would He approve of my flirting with that married man at the gym?* We forget that He's there watching anyway. If we could see Him there, would our decisions seem so innocent? You may think I'm being petty, but remember, vile acts of impurity are always preceded by other, smaller factors that set the stage for them. How can I keep my *way* pure if I'm not keeping my conversation pure? How can I keep my thoughts pure if I'm habitually listening to music or watching things that keep sexual, provocative thoughts and images before me?

Many people are walking in cycles of failure, because they've never settled the deep heart issues. Instead, they make a surface decision, fingers crossed, hoping they can say "no" the next time temptation presents itself. But temptation presents itself daily in these smaller ways, and our daily decisions in the small things affect the choices we will make in the big things. Jesus said,

> Blessed are the pure **in heart**, for they shall see God (Matthew 5:8 ESV).

When purity is established in our hearts, it will overflow and affect all areas of our lives.

My goal in all of this is not to condemn you, but to inspire you to make daily choices to walk in purity, not because someone screamed at you that you're supposed to, but because you recognize the necessity and value of it for your own sake.

SOME RULES ARE MEANT NOT TO BE BROKEN

A lot of times, people disobey or break rules because they don't understand the purpose or the heart behind them. In the case of purity, we as the church have been very effective at handing out the rules but pretty ineffective at explaining the "why" behind them. It's just not good enough to say, "Choose abstinence, so you don't get pregnant or contract an STD." Those are head arguments, and while they may work for a time, they are usually no match for raging hormones in the heat of the moment. However, when we understand the heart of our Father, then we can move past head arguments and to the heart issues. That's where we begin to realize that when God gives us rules and boundaries, they are for our own good.

Growing up, I gained a healthy respect for rules. I realize that if you grew up in an overly harsh environment with many unexplained and unrealistic expectations, you may have grown up hating rules. On the other hand, maybe you grew up in a free-for-all home where there was no structure at all. In our home, there were established rules that were clearly given from a place of love and protection. I knew what the rules were, and most of the time, I knew *why* they were. Even when I didn't like them, I understood that the rules were there for my good.

One of my early childhood memories is from when I was about 5 years old; I was told that a little girl from our daycare had been hit by a car and killed. After that, I never questioned the rule of having to hold an adult's hand any time I crossed a street. I was okay sacrificing my false sense of "freedom" – the ability to run wherever I wanted whenever I wanted – in order to have a greater sense of safety, to be protected from unseen danger. I knew that there were some places I could run and play uninhibited, like in the large, fenced-in backyard, but in potentially unsafe places, I was more than willing to stay near an adult. I gained a keen awareness early on that rules were there for my safety, not to squelch my fun. So whether I liked the rules or not, I knew the place the rules came from was ultimately one of love and protection.

Similarly, God's rules about sex, purity, and marriage are not there to steal our fun or to take away our freedom. They are there to protect us. Essentially, God gives us this huge, wide, fenced-in yard called "marriage," in which we can enjoy sex freely. All other territories are considered unsafe, and – for our own good – He strictly forbids us from entering into sex in any other context besides marriage. Let's look at some specific examples:

> *When you follow the desires of your sinful nature, the results are very clear: sexual immorality, impurity, lustful pleasures, idolatry, sorcery, hostility, quarreling, jealousy, outbursts of anger, selfish ambition, dissension, division, envy, drunkenness, wild parties, and other sins like these.*

Let me tell you again, as I have before, that anyone living that sort of life will not inherit the Kingdom of God (Galatians 5:19 – 21 NLT).

➢ *Yes, I am afraid that when I come … I will be grieved because many of you have not given up your old sins. You have not repented of your impurity, sexual immorality, and eagerness for lustful pleasure* (2 Corinthians 12:21 NLT).

➢ *… Don't fool yourselves. Those who indulge in sexual sin, or who worship idols, or commit adultery, or are male prostitutes, or practice homosexuality, or are thieves, or greedy people, or drunkards, or are abusive, or cheat people – none of these will inherit the Kingdom of God* (1 Corinthians 6:9 – 10 NLT).

Wow, to say the least, the Apostle Paul is pretty straightforward here, isn't he? We can't leave this last Scripture passage, though, without letting you in on the hope he offers in the very next verse. This is for anyone who feels like you've already failed, you've already missed the mark:

Some of you were once like that. ***But you were cleansed; you were made holy; you were made right with God*** *by calling on the name of the Lord Jesus Christ and by the Spirit of our God* (v. 11 NLT).

So while the Bible is clear that sexual sin is a serious matter (by the way, so are all the other things mentioned in those verses), the Bible is also clear that we can be ***cleansed*** from all previous impurity simply by calling on the Name of Jesus.

IT'S MY BODY

Wrong. False. Totally untrue. I know that's a big thing to a lot of people, acting like they have complete freedom to do whatever they want with whomever they want, because it's their body. The Apostle Paul sets the record straight on that, too:

> You say, "I am allowed to do anything" – but not everything is good for you. And even though "I am allowed to do anything," I must not become a slave to anything... But you can't say that our bodies were made for sexual immorality. **They were made for the Lord, and the Lord cares about our bodies...**
>
> Don't you realize that **your bodies are actually parts of Christ**? Should a man take his body, which is part of Christ, and join it to a prostitute? Never! And don't you realize that if a man joins himself to a prostitute, **he becomes one body with her**? For the Scriptures say, "The two are united into one." But the person who is joined to the Lord is one spirit with him.
>
> Run from sexual sin! No other sin so clearly affects the body as this one does. For sexual immorality is a sin against your own body. Don't you realize that your body is the temple of the Holy Spirit, who lives in you and was given to you by God? **You do not belong to yourself, for God bought you with a high price. So you must honor God with your body** (1 Corinthians 6:12 – 20 NLT).

When we violate God's laws regarding sex, we are actually violating *ourselves*. When we join with another person in sex,

163

we bind ourselves to that person – we become "one" with them. That's why there is no such thing as casual sex. It's not possible to have a one-night stand with someone, because whether you know it or not, you will each carry the other one with you from that encounter into the rest of your lives. This is extremely unhealthy and damaging when it occurs outside of marriage. The only human being you are meant to be sexually united with is your marriage partner – for us ladies, that means our husbands and no one else. Within marriage, the unseen bonds created by sex are healthy and intentional, put there by God; outside of marriage, those bonds enslave and harm us. Let me give you a literal but lighthearted example of what I mean.

I used to have two cute little Yorkshire Terriers, and they were both a joy and a mess at the same time! The younger of the two dogs, Jackson, was a pretty hyper little puppy, so it was challenging trying to teach him how to walk on a leash. To train him to stay with me, I would attach one end of his leash to him and the other end to my ankle, keeping him with me as we walked through the house. As adorable as he was, Jackson wasn't always the smartest that he could have been. When he wasn't paying attention to me, he would walk off in the opposite direction, resulting of course in the inevitable, unexpected *yank* when he reached the end of the slack in the leash. He would jerk back unexpectedly (thankfully, he was only about 5 pounds, so it didn't knock me off-balance at all, but it didn't hurt him, either). The only way Jackson could avoid being yanked around was to focus on me, to walk with me, and even to anticipate my every move.

Now let's take a light example and relate it to the deep topic at hand. When you sleep with someone, you're attaching yourself to that person. When you try to go your separate ways, those attachments don't just go away. As a result, in some way or another – emotionally, mentally, maybe even spiritually – you end up being yanked around. The only One who can break those connections between you and past sexual partners is Jesus Christ. But believe me, He *can* and *will*, if you ask Him.

Think of the path of purity as if Jackson had finally put two and two together and started walking with me instead of against me. When we attach ourselves first to God, when we learn to walk with Him, to focus on Him, to pay attention to His every move, then we can walk not only in peace but in safety, right next to Him in His shadow – and as an added bonus, we'll probably stop feeling like life is jerking us around so much! Then, in that place of safety, He can connect us to another person – a future husband, perhaps – who is also connected to Him, watching His every move, focusing on God first.

When God connects two people together who are connected to Him, then their marriage will be headed in the same direction. They can walk in unity, and – once married – the sexual bond between them will only strengthen the power of their union, rather than compete with it.

When we understand God's principles and His heart of love for protecting us, then we can position ourselves to walk in the path of purity intentionally and reverently, instead of just rolling the dice and hoping we can make it. But what about those among us whose purity was lost a long time ago?

INTERRUPTED INNOCENCE

Sex doesn't just happen. Many young women have shared with me their stories of pasts filled with promiscuity and careless sex, but their stories never start with a random decision to sleep with someone. In every single case, other events, decisions, or behaviors preceded and set the stage for their actions long before they gave up on their path to purity. Something affected their self-image, their perception of men and sex, and even their perception of God. Their innocence was compromised in one way or another long before they willingly gave themselves to someone.

Do you remember Maddie from Chapter Three? Maddie may be a made-up character, but the components of her story are all too real. Like Maddie, many young girls never had a strong father-figure, and in many cases, sick-minded men took advantage of them when they were young. In other cases, young girls were exposed to pornography or were made to lie in the same room, trying not to watch or hear while their mother allowed various men into her bed. Before they were even old enough to make decisions about sex and purity, precious daughters were exposed to sex in an unhealthy and perverted way, they were devalued in their own eyes, and any concept of innocence they had was shattered.

The enemy knows that purity is powerful, so it's really no wonder that he launched an all-out attack against us, God's daughters, in this area. One thing is sure: The enemy does not fight fairly. He plays dirty. Remember, you and I remind him of the One who both decreed and secured his eternal defeat. The enemy is indeed defeated, but he still goes to horrific

extremes to try to convince us that we are defeat
why Jesus said:

> *The thief comes only to steal and kill and destroy; I have come that they may have life, and have it to the full* (John 10:10).

It is important for us to recognize that no matter what we have been through – whether by choice or by violation of our will – any attempts to steal our innocence have been launched by "the thief" Jesus described in this verse. The enemy, the devil, is the one ultimately behind these attacks, and no matter how subtle or how severe, every attack was his attempt to *steal* our purity, *kill* our dreams, and *destroy* our futures.

THE ESSENCE OF GRACE

Let's read that verse from earlier again: "Blessed are the pure in heart, for they shall see God." I love that Jesus specifically says, "the pure *in heart*," because this shows me that even if I have lost purity in my body at some point along the way, He is looking at my heart. His Grace covers my failures, if only I present my heart to Him and allow Him to make it pure again. How do I do that? 1 John 1:9 promises us:

> *If we confess our sins, he is faithful and just and will forgive us our sins and purify us from all unrighteousness.*

God always looks at the heart.

When we come in our brokenness and confess our sins of impurity, asking Him to forgive us – when we present the

167

pieces of our heart to Him and ask Him to purify us and make us whole – He *does.*

Remember, it always comes back to the Father's heart for us. It always comes back to the Father's Love for *you.* He will never turn you away, no matter how ugly your past is, no matter how torn your life is, no matter how impure your body, mind, or spirit has been.

In just one moment, He can turn everything around, and He can purify you from all unrighteousness, whether that be unrighteousness you chose or unrighteousness that was forced on you. Either way, He purifies. He cleanses. He makes all things new.

> *Therefore, if anyone is in Christ, he is a new creation; old things have passed away; behold, all things have become new* (2 Corinthians 5:17 NKJV).

No matter what you have been through, you must realize that **His Grace is greater than your failures. It's greater than your circumstances. It's greater than your pain. His Grace is enough.**

Grace restores you from wherever you are now, from wherever you've ever been, to a place of purity. Grace puts that weapon back in your hand, so you can move forward as if you had never let it go, as if it had never been taken away.

If you want to take hold of this Grace for your own life, keep reading, because we're about to do exactly that.

FIRST THINGS FIRST

Daughters of Jerusalem, I charge you:
Do not arouse or awaken love until it so desires.
Song of Solomon 8:4

First things first. In order to walk in purity, you have to get back to square one, get back to a place of purity. For many, that means wiping the slate clean from a past filled with abuse, violation, and self-destructive decisions. Hear the urgency of the charge in Song of Solomon: "Do not arouse or awaken love until it so desires." There is obviously a right time and a wrong time for desires to be wakened in us, and as we discussed, many of us have unfortunately had those desires wakened before the time God intended.

If that's where you are, then before we go any further with the practical steps, I want to invite you to pray. Let's get the heart issue taken care of first. If you need help knowing what to say, I invite you to pray as much of this prayer that applies to you. If you've never invited Jesus into your life, if you did at one point but feel you need to re-surrender and make things right with Him, or if you already have a relationship with Christ but need freedom from a past of impurity, then this is for you:

Dear God,

I am here before You, asking You to forgive me of my sins. I repent to You for all of the things I have done that were against You; please take away my guilt and shame. I believe that You sent Your Son, Jesus, to the earth to die for my sins and to rise again from the dead to give me victory!

Please lead my life, be my Father, my Lord and Savior, and my ever-present help. I receive Your forgiveness, and I surrender all to You, including my spirit, soul, and body.

Father, as Your daughter, I ask You to cleanse me from all impurity, specifically sexual impurity. Please wash my heart, mind, spirit, and even my body by Your powerful Grace. Please restore to me my innocence before You. I ask You to help me to forgive all who violated me, whether they knew what they were doing or not. As I receive Your forgiveness for myself, I choose to forgive others completely. I ask You to destroy the unhealthy, unseen bonds that were established between them and me. Please cause anything that has been prematurely awakened in me – in my desires, my physical body, and my mind – to be put back to sleep until You decide it is time to awaken these things in me in a pure way, when You unite me to my future husband in marriage.

I thank You, Father, that even though You didn't cause any of those bad things to happen to me, You have always been looking out for me, guiding me to this moment right now, where I can join with You and walk connected to You from this day forward.

I receive Your Grace, Your peace, and Your Love for me. Thank You for making me new.

In Jesus' Name,

Amen.

If you prayed that, I have no doubt that God heard you and is meeting you right now, wherever you are, with His Love and His Presence! I'm grateful with you for the power that only He holds to give us a brand new start!

THE PATH OF PURITY

Simply put, the path of purity involves:

1. **A position of your heart.**

2. **A pattern of daily decisions.**

3. **A process of renewing your mind.**

We now know that purity begins and flows from the heart. It comes from a heart that is positioned toward God, because truly, there is no purity outside of Him.

Secondly, walking in Purity must be a pattern of daily decisions that lead us along the right path. Honestly, these decisions have a lot to do with common sense! No matter what "weapon" of self-defense you may choose in dangerous situations, I think we would all agree that the best weapon is to stay out of danger's path in the first place! Common sense is the series of decisions that help us to avoid danger's path, both literally and figuratively. I am not suggesting that we should be paranoid or live in fear, but we should live in heightened awareness, spiritually and naturally speaking. **A huge part of walking in purity is eliminating the *opportunity* for impurity to develop.**

Purity is an active choice, not a passive one. Remember, you must *guard* your *way* according to God's Word.

You may think that what I'm about to say is impractical or extreme, but I urge you to think it through before you dismiss it, and evaluate for your own life what measures you might need to implement for your own protection. To give you ideas, here are some practical examples of protective decisions I have made for my own path of purity:

- ➢ I avoid walking in parking lots alone at night. If that's not possible, then I look for well-lit parking spots, make sure other people are nearby, and keep my keys in my hand with my thumb on the alarm button. I walk with my head up, staying aware of my surroundings.

- ➢ I don't go to a guy's house/apartment alone. It doesn't matter how godly he is or how godly I am. This isn't just to avoid physical danger. From an integrity standpoint as a single Christian, it doesn't look good for me to be in a guy's home by myself, and it can create all sorts of *opportunities* for temptation, impurity, and damage to my reputation.

- ➢ I don't let guys/men into my house/apartment if nobody else is home.

- ➢ Guys are never allowed in my bedroom. Period.

- ➢ I don't hang out in places where purity is blatantly dishonored. You're not going to find me at a club or a bar or a crazy party. You're not going to find me hanging around people who are getting drunk and losing all sense of good decision-making. It's not that I'm better than they are; it's just that their bad decisions can affect me, and I'm just not willing to give anyone the *opportunity* to do that.

> ➢ I don't develop online friendships or relationships with people I don't personally know. There are tons of predators out there, and I'm not giving them any *opportunity* to make me their prey.

These are just some examples of choices I've made to protect my path. Again, you may think it is extreme, but you can control a lot more than you think you can by controlling your surroundings. Purity can be much easier to walk in when we simply eliminate opportunities for impurity to invade our lives. Temptation is much easier to resist when you don't put yourself in the position to be tempted in the first place.

Lastly, purity is a process of renewing our minds. Romans 12:2 reminds us:

> *Don't copy the behavior and customs of this world, but let God transform you into a new person **by changing the way you think...** (NLT).*

Our minds must think the God-kind of thoughts. We cannot think lustful thoughts and expect to live out a pure path.

Philippians 4:8 gives us a great model for testing our thoughts:

> *And now, dear brothers and sisters, one final thing. Fix your thoughts on what is true, and honorable, and right,*

and pure, and lovely, and admirable. Think about things that are excellent and worthy of praise (NLT).

I challenge you, as you go throughout your day, to put every thought you have about the opposite sex on trial. Ask yourself, "Was that thought true, honorable, right, pure, lovely, and admirable?" If not, then take authority over it and cast it out. **You have power over your thought life** (2 Corinthians 10:5). Just because a thought tries to come in doesn't mean you have to let it stay there. It is not a sin when an impure thought tries to enter your mind; it is only a sin when you choose to embrace it, think it over, and dwell on it.

THE POSSIBILITIES OF PURITY

As we end this chapter, I hope you are encouraged, filled with hope, optimism, and even faith for the journey ahead! I hope you see the power that purity can play in your life, the protection that it is for you, and all of the possibilities that it holds. Above all, I hope you have found a renewed place on which to stand, both before your Father God and as you face the world before you. All of the power of purity is at your fingertips. Let's join together, rise up, and walk in that power!

Chapter Eleven
WHY MARRIAGE MATTERS

Marriage. Who needs it? At least, most of us have probably been tempted to think that at some point along the way in our struggle with Single.

Besides, we live in a society that seems to be moving further and further away from valuing marriage. I mean, when you look at things logically, why not just move in together and try this thing out before getting married? Why not split the financial burden of an apartment and utilities and vehicles? Why not give the relationship a trial run before we actually commit? So many entities now recognize your "significant other" or "common law companion" as having virtually the same rights as a spouse would anyway, so why bother?

Then when you look at things emotionally, why is marriage so important if so many marriages of those close to you have failed? If your own family has been rampaged by divorce, then why would you even want to go near marriage? For that matter, who defines what marriage is anyway?

We need to talk honestly about these kinds of questions, because they are very prominent now in our generation. But to help us lay a foundation so that we can tackle these issues, we first need to understand what God thinks about marriage. And you probably know me well enough by now to guess what I'm going to do: I can think of no better place to start discovering God's intentions for marriage than the first actual husband-and-wife duo. So once more, let's go right back to the Garden of Eden.

A REFLECTION OF GOD

We've reiterated over and over in our journey together that God made us in His own image (Genesis 1:27). Sometimes we read through the Creation story pretty quickly, maybe even flippantly, because we've heard it all before. I think at times like now, however, it warrants a much closer look. If we can understand God's intentions behind what He did when He created humanity in the first place, then we can better understand not only our value in His eyes, but also how He planned for us to interact with Himself and with one another here on earth. So let's cover some ground together that is, again, foundational and critical to understanding the heart of God in these matters.

Genesis lets us in on God's conversation in heaven when He decided to make humanity. You can imagine that God the Father, Jesus, and the Holy Spirit are talking amongst themselves:

> *Then God said, "Let us make human beings in our image, to be like us..."*

> *So God created human beings in his own image. In the image of God he created them; male and female he created them (Genesis 1:26 – 27 NLT).*

This verse ties us directly to our Creator, because it shows us that He created us as individuals to reflect His likeness in the earth. What we often miss, however, is that our reflection of Him doesn't stop just with each one of us as individuals.

When God wanted to show humans what our relationship with Him can look like, He painted a picture using relationships we could see and understand. In other words, He knew that there would be times it would be hard for us to wrap our heads around relating to an unseen Being, so He wanted to give us some visible, tangible examples to help us understand. He gave us two types of relationships that most closely reflect what our relationship with Him should look like. One is that of parent and child, which we have looked at in-depth along our journey so far; the other is that of a husband and wife.

When God created the world we know, the first human relationship He established was that of a man and wife – marriage. He didn't start out by giving Adam a buddy to hang out with. He didn't start out by giving Adam a colleague or an employee or even a son. God started out by giving Adam a wife (Genesis 2:21 – 25). The next human relationship He gave them was the special bond between parents and children (Genesis 4:1 – 2). God established the family first, because His plan was that the family would cultivate life and fruitfulness throughout the earth (Genesis 1:28), and that the family itself would become a natural, real-world reflection of God's own family – us.

See, not only does the Bible tell us that we are made in God's image, but it also shows us how we are God's children, and as the Church, we are Jesus' Bride. In the New Testament, the Apostle Paul makes both connections for us:

> So in Christ Jesus you are all children of God through faith (Galatians 3:26).

> ... *"A man leaves his father and mother and is joined to his wife, and the two are united into one." This is a great mystery, but it is an illustration of the way Christ and the church are one* (Ephesians 5:31-32 NLT).

Why am I going to all of this detail? I want each of us to understand that God is a God of relationship. He holds dearly His relationship with each one of us, and He values highly the relationships He established for us in the beginning: marriage and family.

OUR CURRENT CONDITION

With this knowledge in mind, it's no wonder that our present culture has seen such a great attack against marriage and the family. I'm not talking politics; I'm speaking of spiritual attack here. Just think about it. The value of marriage in the eyes of our culture has taken a huge hit. Soaring divorce rates, the relatively new popularity of co-habitation, and the widespread degree of single-parenting are some of the reasons I believe our culture has pushed marriage to the back burner.

Even so, I have to look beyond the culture itself and try to pinpoint what's going on underneath the surface. With so many absent fathers, struggling mothers, abandoned children, and broken homes, wouldn't it be easy for the enemy, the devil, to think he has achieved the upper-hand in destroying God's plan for marriage and the family? After all, **if the enemy can destroy our perception of marriage and family, then he can greatly hinder our ability to relate to God our Father.** It's no surprise that the family has been under attack for generations. It's hard to relate to a heavenly Father if you've had no good example of a true earthly father; it's hard to understand covenant, unconditional Love if you've never known a marriage that displayed undying commitment and really succeeded in the long run.

Remember, satan hates all things God. His beef isn't even really with you and me; it's with God, and the fact is, we remind him of God. Marriage and the family are further reminders to him of the perfection God created, of the relationships God established. I told you before; satan doesn't fight fairly. He constantly tries to use God's children to get to God. So see, if he can destroy how we see marriage, if he can destroy the healthy nature of a parent-child relationship, if he can break up homes and cause us to be unable to understand what marriage and family were really supposed to be, then he can drive wedges between God and us, God's children.

Maybe you've not been able to understand the true heart of our Father, because your own relationship with your father was either fragmented, destructive, or non-existent. Do you see now that God didn't do that to you? The enemy tried to use a set of bad circumstances, mixed with decisions made by imperfect people, to separate you from God your Father. The problem with his plan is that now your eyes are opening, and you're beginning to see that *nothing* can separate you from your Father's love (Romans 8:38 – 39).

Ultimately, we need to understand that marriage is a spiritual matter, not a matter of opinion and not a matter of politics. God created marriage very specifically, intentionally, and lovingly, and nothing our culture does is going to change God's institution of marriage. Understanding that, let's try to address some of the questions we hit so often nowadays.

LOGIC VS. WISDOM

First of all, logically, it might be hard to argue with some of the questions we asked earlier: *Why not move in together to save money? Why not try things out first? We're committed to each other anyway; we don't need a legal document to prove it.* The problem is that, no matter how logical your argument may be, logic falls so short in the grand scheme of things. **Logic considers only what we see. Wisdom considers both the seen (our world) and the unseen (God's world).** What do I mean by that?

Sure, Logic says, "If we can move in together and save a bunch of money, we can buy our first house and be way better off than most couples."

Wisdom, however, knows that there are more factors to moving in together than just finances. Wisdom also knows that finances aren't a justification for doing whatever we want to do. Unfortunately, I've watched way too many people rationalize their way into bad decisions. Just because you can rationalize the logic for it in your mind does not mean it's a wise decision all-around.

Ephesians 5:15 urges us, "See then that you walk circumspectly, not as fools but as wise" (NKJV). When you think about the word "circumspectly," think about the circumference of a circle – the outer edge of it. If you're checking out a new car, you walk around the perimeter of the car; you walk in a circle around it, observing every aspect of it inside and out before making your decision. This is how we are to walk through our lives, looking at things from every angle, anchored in God's viewpoint, considering the big picture and not just the obvious details right in front of us.

Wisdom considers not only the physical and financial aspects, but it also factors in the mental, emotional, relational, and especially spiritual repercussions that we so often forget or outright refuse to consider. Wisdom also considers God's rules and instructions, even when we don't understand them. Wisdom knows they are there for our own good. Logic says that physical, tangible facts are the main thing; **Wisdom knows that ignoring God's spiritual laws and pretending they don't exist doesn't make them go away.**

This may sound cliché, but you can pretend all day long that gravity isn't a real thing; you can even refuse to believe it exists. Your refusal to acknowledge it does not exempt you from its power. Gravity is a physical law God has set in place, and we are all bound to it, like it or not. If you defy it, God isn't going to punish you by striking you with lightning. However, neither is He going to release you from the boundaries of it. So if you get in your mind that you're going to jump off a skyscraper and fly, just because you refuse to be bound by gravity, well, then you'd better be strapped to something that *is* able to fly via physics and science (other laws God has put in place); if not, your physical body is still going to respond to the law of gravity the way everyone else's does. Falling flat on the pavement is not a result of God's punishing you; it's a result of your ignoring the laws He put in place and blindly moving ahead in your own ignorance or stubbornness.

Like the physical laws He has set in place, God has instituted spiritual laws that we are not exempt from just because we may be ignorant of them or pretend they aren't real.

Again, we must realize that **God's laws for us come from a place of Love and not from a place of manipulative control.** We sometimes get an image of God as if He is a control freak who doesn't want us to have any fun. This is not the God I know.

As we discussed in the previous chapter, a true father knows that rules are not only good but are necessary for the protection of his family. In spite of a growing trend to let kids be "free" and make their own decisions and explore the world around them uninhibited, some rules and structure are imperative for healthy growth and development. Even beyond childhood, boundaries are a good thing to help us navigate life successfully. We have structure to our roads, guardrails to keep us from driving off the deep end, lanes to keep us from running into one another. Boundaries are a really good thing!

Any law or rule that God has implemented has been done so from a place of sheer, protective love for us. When we see His love for us, we realize that there's really no justification for our rebel streak that just wants to be different and live outside the box. Who wants to live outside of His love for us?

Logic may be able to argue against God's rules, but Wisdom always accounts for the Father's good intentions toward us. So with a heart seeking Wisdom, let's look at some of these spiritual laws – protective boundaries – our Father has given us about marriage.

WHAT THE BIBLE REALLY SAYS

First of all, like we've already explored from Genesis, the Bible is clear about God's design for marriage in the very beginning. He literally created one woman for one man, for them to be husband and wife. He gave us this model as His intention for us: One man married to one woman, intimately connected in the covenant of marriage, a relationship surpassed nowhere else in history besides Christ's unfailing love for His Church. No other human-to-human relationship can parallel marriage as God intended it. There's nothing else like it! God sealed His intentions in Genesis 2:24, "Therefore a man shall leave his father and mother and be joined to his wife, and they shall become one flesh" (NKJV).

We find God's definition of marriage reiterated in the New Testament: "...each man should have his own wife, and each woman should have her own husband" (1 Corinthians 7:2 NLT).

Hebrews 13:4 clearly says, "Marriage should be honored by all, and the marriage bed kept pure, for God will judge the adulterer and all the sexually immoral." God designed marriage to be filled with honor, purity, and faithfulness.

Notice that it says "Marriage should be honored by all..." It doesn't say we only honor marriage once we're married! All of us are called to honor marriage regardless of our current position in life. God has set in place the spiritual law that sex is only for marriage (Proverbs 5:15 – 17). It's not just a suggestion; it's a *law* that, when violated, carries repercussions as real as if we had tried to violate gravity.

It doesn't matter how much you may rationalize that you could just live together and try each other out; if you're having sex outside of marriage, you're setting yourselves up for spiritual disaster. *But what if we're not having sex?* I don't hear this often, and I'll be honest; if I do hear this, I raise my eyebrows in skepticism, because I'm not sure how two people deeply attracted to one another can live with each other and still maintain a pure lifestyle. But for the sake of argument, let's say that you are. Three thoughts come to my mind:

1. Remember that path of purity we talked about? Living together is creating all kinds of *opportunity* for you to plunge off of that path and into sexual sin with one another. When you lead one another into impurity, what is left other than feelings of guilt, failure, and distrust created between the two of you? Why would you want to expose your relationship to that kind of risk?

2. Even if you both happen to be the two people in the world with the willpower of steel and are able to live together, right there in the same house, without compromising your purity, people are going to assume that you are sexually active. How many couples do you know who live together and remain chaste? Point made. So even if you're not doing anything wrong, you're giving the appearance that you are doing something wrong. You can say all day long that you don't care about other people's opinions, but you should care, at the very least, about your own integrity. 1 Thessalonians 5:22 says, "Abstain from all appearance of evil" (KJV). In other words, don't even give people

room to question your motives and actions. It's not about living under people's scrutiny or bowing down to judgments of others. Somebody is watching you – whether it be a younger sister, a young professional you're mentoring, or a young person in your church – and your reputation is a huge part of your testimony to those people. Even if what you're doing isn't wrong in your own eyes, your actions and life choices will either support or contradict your claim that you love God and follow Christ. We've already read where Paul warned us that just because something is permissible (you can get away with it without directly violating God's law) doesn't mean it's beneficial (1 Corinthians 10:23 – 24).

3. My last thought is this, and it's simply based in a romantic notion I have: Why would you want to "play house" before you're actually committed to one another in marriage? Isn't part of the fun of wedding planning the part where you get to plan your life together *after* the wedding? Why jump in and do all of that ahead of time? To me, that's like stealing your own thunder. It's like opening your presents before Christmas. Sure, it may be fun today, but it's stealing a little bit of the joy you could have had when your special moment does arrive.

So whatever your rationale, the bottom line is this: **Trying to experience the benefits of marriage without being married is a recipe for failure.**

So what if you're already living together? What do you do if you want to go back and change things? Well, obviously, you can't undo what you've already experienced, but you can make things right, both before God, with one another, and in your physical circumstances. Few people have my respect to the degree of my friends who have made hard decisions, moved out from their boyfriends' apartments (or made their boyfriends move out), and put enough space between them to allow purity to breathe in their relationship again. In some cases, the boyfriend throws a big-boy temper tantrum and ends the relationship; in other cases, he respects his girlfriend's (or fiancée's) choice and honors her request to follow purity. If you're afraid he would leave you over such a decision, then I would have to ask you to think about what your relationship is really founded on in the first place. If you make the tough decisions, just know that your Father God will honor your decisions and bless you for them, regardless of how your boyfriend responds.

WISDOM WINS EVERY TIME

So back to that whole Wisdom vs. Logic thing we were talking about earlier. Now that we know the expectations (boundaries, laws, rules) that God set in place, and now that we know He did so out of His boundless Love for us, we can return to our original discussion and lay to rest all of Logic's arguments.

Like we discussed earlier, Logic only considers cold, hard facts that we can feel, see, hear, smell, and taste. It considers the bank account, how to make ends meet, how to rationalize the decision. Logic may even consider some emotional aspects. The problem is that, while Wisdom does consider Logic (Wisdom never ignores common sense), Logic in and of itself is inadequate as a director in life. Logic gives first consideration to the facts in front of us and what we *want*, and it gives secondary consideration – if any at all – to what the Bible says. Logic will even twist what the Bible says around to try to justify that what we want is okay. Wisdom, however, gives first consideration to God's ways, then incorporates Logic to the extent that it fits into God's ways. This is the only way to come up with a decision that honors God and protects us in the long run.

Our fallible human Logic simply doesn't understand the unseen effects of defying God's laws. Logic doesn't know that living in a committed-but-not-quite-committed environment will take its toll on you emotionally and mentally over time. Logic doesn't understand that if you're living together and sleeping together, then not only is that a destructive lifestyle of sin, but it also is forming unholy, ungodly bonds between you and this person you supposedly love. If you really love each other, why would you want to let this spiritual ugliness enter your relationship? If not for your own sake, then for the sake of this special person in your life, wouldn't you want to do things God's ways?

CLEAR YOUR CACHE

Even though society has allowed its perception of marriage to be eroded over time, this is not God's intention for marriage. This is not the *honor* described in Hebrews 13:4. Look at the way the Amplified Bible puts the same verse:

Let marriage be held in honor (esteemed worthy, precious, of great price, and especially dear) in all things. And thus let the marriage bed be undefiled...

It's time for us to clear our mental cache in how we've perceived marriage. Refresh the browser, so-to-speak, and do away with all of the ungodly mutations of marriage that our society has presented to us. It's time to do a factory reset in our minds and emotions, embracing God's intention of what marriage is really supposed to be for us.

God has given us marriage as a protective covenant, a place in which two people can find refuge, covering, intimacy, and strength. Marriage is meant to be a display of the power that exists when two people, joined together by God, enter into agreement and unity together in a commitment that no one can break. Jesus Himself said, "...Since they are no longer two but one, let no one split apart what God has joined together" (Mark 10:8-9 NLT).

This is your Father's dream for you regarding marriage. If you will be married one day, you need to know now that as much as you may have dreamt about it for yourself, He wants it for you even more than you could imagine! Your Father wants you to know this kind of love that perseveres past the romantic feelings, past the honeymoon phase, and past the trials in life – a love that overcomes. He wants you to know this likeness of His perfect Love, in the presence of which fear cannot stand.

God's design for marriage is to be a reflection of His relationship with *you*.

Imagine the beauty of a marriage in which both of you have this kind of intimate relationship with God. It is not a problem-free marriage, so don't allow yourself to be disillusioned. It's a love that conquers all. When Perfect Love is the center of your relationship, nothing is too great to overcome.

So the next time you find yourself asking why marriage matters, ask yourself, *Why would I want to settle for anything less?*

Chapter Twelve
FINDING THE ONE

Dear Son,

I watch you as you play, as you grow and learn day by day. Your innocence, your love for life, and your sincerity all astound me, and I cherish your boyish playfulness. Even as I enjoy every moment of your childhood, I know that manhood is coming. Some mothers might be afraid of their boys growing into men, but I am not, for I know that you are growing as a man of God.

*Since before you were born, I have prayed for you and for the wife God will bring to you one day. My son, you need to know a few things about her ahead of time, so that when you begin to look for her one day, you will be able to recognize her, and perhaps more importantly, you will be able to recognize who is not her. First, you need to know that **not just anybody can be the wife God has for you.** There are many women out there who don't take life seriously, who aren't well-rooted in God's love for them, or who have no concept of the call of God on their lives. These women cannot walk with you. In fact, **there will be more women who can't walk with you than who can.** Don't be discouraged when it feels like the options are few. You aren't supposed to settle for just whoever will have you. God has someone incredibly, specifically tailor-made to walk side-by-side with you, and He has made you incredibly, specifically tailor-made to walk with her.*

In fact, having few options will actually make your search easier if you'll let it. You'll be free to ignore the advances of seductive, ill-intentioned women, because you will recognize immediately that the woman of God you are looking for would not act like that. You will stay free from the lures of manipulative, controlling women, because by being secure in who you are in the Lord, you will recognize that you do not belong in a relationship with one of them. Instead of wasting months and even years dating women who only know how to use men to alleviate their own insecurities, and instead of wasting time in relationships that have no future, you will be free to focus on your calling. You will be free to enjoy the journey while trusting the Lord to lead you in every step that you take. Having fewer options, my son, is actually liberating, because it will spare you much heartache of pursuing relationships with those who are not to be pursued by you. In the end, you will be thankful that the options were few.

*Second, I want you to understand that **beauty is everything.** But let me be clear: I want you to know what beauty looks like. The beauty your soul longs for in a wife is not just physical. It's inside, outside, all around – It's everything. If you find your heart drifting toward a beautiful woman, I urge you to pause, step back, and make sure she is truly beautiful in every way. A truly beautiful woman regards others with love and respect. She will treat her parents with honor. She will understand and submit to authority in her life. She may be fun and spontaneous and energetic, or she may be calm and introspective and gentle, but in either case, when it comes down to life and her future, she will take the things of God seriously.*

Third, if you bring a girl home to meet us, you need to know I will be watching to see how she treats you. We are raising you to be a man deserving of respect and honor. A woman who cannot give you that is either not the one for you or has a lot of maturing to do before she can become the one.

Just remember, dear boy, that when the day comes and you begin looking for your wife, the Holy Spirit will guide you as much as you will let Him, and your father and I will give you counsel as often as you will ask us. Trust God's timing. He will lead you to her when you are both ready.

I love you as big as the world and more,

Mom

ARE YOU BECOMING *THE ONE* FOR SOMEONE?

So often in this journey of Single, we think about what "I've always dreamed of," what "I am asking God for," who "I pray God will bring me" – I, I, I – Even in trying to focus on God, it's really still all about us, isn't it? The journey of Single is a tricky one in that it is very, very easy for those of us on this path to fall into the trap of self-centeredness. Despite our best intentions in trying to focus on God, when it comes down to this lifelong spouse thing, it's so hard *not* to think about ourselves, isn't it?!

I shared the letter above, because I believe it will do us good to think about our future marriage from someone's perspective other than our own. What if it was your spouse's mother who wrote that letter to her son many years ago? What if his parents have been praying for you all these years? What if his mom prayed that her son will find a woman who is secure in her relationship with God, confident of who she is, and respectful of others?

Think about it. Are you letting God shape *you* into the kind of woman you would want for your son one day? Or are you so consumed with your own state of loneliness that you have found it difficult to allow God to penetrate the deepest parts of your heart and life? Are you a fragile, broken woman looking desperately for a rescuer in a man, or are you the kind of restored, healthy woman who can link arms and walk with a man of God in the destiny God has for both of you?

Instead of thinking only about what *we* want, what *we* need, what *we've* always dreamed of, what if we stopped and looked from the perspective of what *he* will need, what *he's* asking God for, what *he* is looking for?

If I'm asking God for a Prince, am I doing my part to become the Princess he will want to marry?

If we're going to find the right one (and avoid falling for the wrong ones along the way), then we're going to have to look beyond ourselves, fix our eyes on our Father God, and be willing to let Him guide our search. Let's talk about some principles that can help us do just that.

KEYS TO FINDING THE ONE

Key 1: Stop looking.

Wait, what? That's right. The first step in finding the one is to stop looking. The first thing we need to understand is that no matter what, **we cannot manipulate God into making this happen faster for us!** So instead of trying to memorize some magical formula of how to find our mates, let's just focus on doing this thing God's way.

How many times have you lost something – maybe your keys, or some loose cash, or the remote control – and you turned the house upside down looking for it, with absolutely no success? Then, after you've exhausted all options and have given up, the thing you were looking for turns up somewhere you least expected it.

If you will trust God instead of exhausting all your energy frantically looking, looking, looking, then God will bring you and your spouse together at just the right time – and it might be when you least expect it.

It was a thrilling day for me to realize that I had stopped looking for my husband. I finally realized I had exhausted all viable options in my life for finding my husband, and I got tired of searching, thinking I'd found him, then being disappointed over being wrong – again. One day, it dawned on me that I was totally content waiting on God. It didn't happen overnight, and it didn't mean I had lost the desire to be married one day. It just meant I had this peace and even an excitement about the future, knowing that God and I could enjoy the rest of this season of Single together no matter what.

It was shortly after that day of realization when I decided to pour my energy into writing a book to other women walking through Single with me. My season of Single birthed this book, because I was finally able to turn my attention away from myself to more productive things.

So stop looking and let God surprise you! Meanwhile, there are some other things you can do to prepare yourself for the day that *the one* just shows up unexpectedly.

Key 2: Evict Insecurity.

I realize that some of you read the letter earlier and thought, "If I were his mother, no, I *wouldn't* want my son to marry a girl like me. No, I'm *not* the princess he would want." I realize that many of us aren't secure at all in what we have to offer to our future mates. So let's bring some balance.

The purpose of considering someone else's perspective isn't to beat ourselves up about our own flaws. The point is not to pick ourselves apart. In fact, if we do that, then we aren't accomplishing anything at all.

I'm not projecting onto you an expectation that you become perfect before God will bring you your mate. Actually, let's swing the pendulum the other way for a minute. As much as we ask God for these wonderful, strong men of God, we need to stay grounded in reality and realize that neither these men nor we ourselves will be perfect at that moment when God brings us together. Even in our best-prepared state, we are still talking about humans here. We're all works in progress! God has created us all perfectly, but we are still being perfected in Him. The point of my questions earlier was to help us be less self-centered. However, if you're now focusing on how terribly inadequate you are, then you're still focusing on yourself, aren't you?

We've been through a lot together now in this journey. I hope by now, you understand that as a daughter of God, a daughter of Love Himself, you can be imperfect and still continue to offer God your best every day. When you understand that He loves you no matter what, you can be okay with your imperfections. It doesn't mean you won't try to improve those areas. It just means you aren't held back by them anymore.

Key 3: Target Your Affections.

So often, our hearts get broken because we wildly shoot our affections at whatever moving target we see in front of us (ahem, the random, single guy that smiled at you when he walked by), and we miss our shot and feel like a failure. All the while, we haven't stopped to ask ourselves if what we are shooting at is even worth catching! So when I say, "Target your affections," I mean, slow down and take a good, hard look at what is in front of you before you throw all you have mindlessly to try to get it!

Even while we are not "looking" for our future spouses, we have the responsibility of managing and appropriately targeting our affections. As we've reminded ourselves before, the Bible clearly tells us in Proverbs 4:23 to guard our hearts or, in some translations, to guard our affections. Why? God tells us to guard our hearts, *because* they literally influence every aspect of our lives.

Our steps tend to go in the direction we have set our affections, so if our affections aren't aimed properly, our entire life can become off-kilter. We will gravitate in whatever direction our affections are pointing with such great force that we may even lose sight of life-long dreams and aspirations we once held dear. I have moved those directions many times before, allowing my heart to point in a different direction than God's purpose for me, and each and every time, it has led me to a place of misery and mediocrity that could only be broken by the Grace of God.

To start identifying what really matters, ask yourself these questions:

1. Besides getting married, what is one dream or desire that I know God has given me for my future?

2. What are some qualities or desires that my husband will need to possess in order for me to accomplish that dream? (e.g., He will have to have a stable relationship with God; he will have to want children; he must love giving to help the needy; he will have to be supportive of his wife having a career).

3. What values must he have that are non-negotiables?

   Side note: If you're a follower of Christ, then the very first non-negotiable should be that he also is a devoted follower of Christ. If you allow your heart to fall for someone who doesn't share your faith in Christ, then you are setting yourself up for a long and difficult road ahead, and to be honest, you are defying the Bible's instruction to us in 2 Corinthians 6:14, "Don't team up with those who are unbelievers. How can righteousness be a partner with wickedness? How can light live with darkness?" (NLT). This isn't offered as a suggestion. It is offered as direct instruction. Paul is clear that we are not to enter into marriage with someone who does not follow Christ. Like all of God's principles, it's there for our own protection.

Many guys in my life have been disqualified as potential dating partners, because they did not have a solid relationship with Christ. It doesn't mean they were terrible people; it just meant we couldn't walk together. And I wasn't going to start dating one of them in order to "help lead them to Christ." God has lots of ways of drawing people to Himself. He's not going to call you to defy His Word in order to lead that man to Christ. Follow God's best for you; heed His instruction not to connect yourself to an unbeliever.

What other values are non-negotiable for you? If you came from a family that has been devastated by alcoholism, then it might be important to you that your spouse doesn't drink, even socially. If your father never provided for you and your siblings, then it might be paramount to you that your husband is self-motivated and has a strong work ethic. On the contrary, if your father was a workaholic and was rarely present, you probably want your future spouse to have strong family values.

These are some questions to help you start forming a silhouette in your mind of what to expect in the man who will one day deserve the focus of your affections.

I used to get really, really specific about what I wanted in the man God has for me. I think it's okay to dream and think about different qualities and characteristics we want, but I also think we need to be realistic enough to understand that God knows what we want better than we do. So while it's good to set some non-negotiable standards that line up with God's Word, we need to submit the intricacies of our dreams to God to fulfill as He knows is best. As Proverbs 16:9 says, "We should make plans – counting on God to direct us" (TLB). God is not going to bring you "the perfect man," because, quite frankly, he doesn't exist! But God will bring you the man who is perfect *for you* (and, in turn, for whom *you* are perfect).

Key 4: Actively Recognize Who Is NOT the One.

Targeting your affections, allowing God to form that silhouette in your heart, will help you recognize many men who simply are not able to be the one for you. You can easily recognize imposters who don't line up with what we see in the Bible. The men we are looking for will have a relationship with God (2 Corinthians 6:14), will be pursuing the true qualities of Love (1 Corinthians 13), and will strive to love us as Christ loves the Church (Ephesians 5:25).

Key 5: Appreciate your emotions, but don't trust them.

How many of us have ever had these kinds of thoughts in a new, potential, or budding relationship?

> ➤ *I've never felt this way about anyone before.*

> ➤ *No one has ever made me feel like this before.*

> ➤ *I've never wanted to be with anyone more than I want to be with him.*

Do you see a common thread? We tend to measure the potential of the relationship by how it makes us *feel.* **Using our**

emotions to predict the potential of a relationship is as reliable as looking at a thermometer to predict if it's going to rain. We simply cannot rely on sheer emotions to lead us.

Emotions can be so fickle and deceiving, in spite of our best intentions. I used to talk about my latest crush by saying things like, "This time, it just *feels* different." I've said it several times, and you probably have, too, probably about several different guys. So if I'm relying on the special feeling I get when I'm with this person, then which one of those was right? One thing's for sure; as many crushes as I've had, they couldn't have *all* been the one! So I know my emotions misled me in most, if not all, of those cases. Beyond the surface crushes, I have even allowed my emotions to mislead me to the point that I sincerely believed God had spoken to me and told me that a specific guy was my future husband (and, yes, I believed that about more than one guy, too, so there's no doubt now that I was wrong about hearing God say that).

Don't underestimate the power of emotion, especially when combined with the strong desire for companionship; together, they can be a toxic pairing, luring the woman with even the best intentions off-course.

It doesn't help any that we still battle Hollywood's portrayal of romanticism, so we are influenced to believe our emotions over reality. How many of us really do believe that the first kiss will tell us whether or not the relationship has long-term potential? *Seriously?!* You're going to let the weight of your entire future be determined by the feeling you do or don't get with a single point of physical contact? That's not real life. You can't mindlessly follow your emotions and expect to end up anywhere worth going in life.

You may even struggle with thinking back to that special one that you felt more strongly about than all the rest. You know in your spirit he wasn't God's best for you, but your emotions keep tugging at you, tempting you to ask, *What if things had worked out? What if he's changed? What if we get a second chance?* I've been tempted in the same way. I used to wonder if that was real love I had for that one special person. Thankfully, God's Truth has kept me grounded from letting my heart run away with my head, so to speak. I know deep within me that he can never be the one God has for me. That reality keeps my emotions in check and keeps my trust in God.

With all of this said, please know that emotions are still part of who we are, and they are an incredible gift from God to help us love and enjoy life! I am an emotional person, and I'm thankful for my emotions! However, I am keenly aware that I cannot let my emotions rule me. Emotions are good for many things, but **emotions are simply not a good advisor of direction and destiny.**

Key 6: Understand that change changes everything.

In other words, you can evaluate the health and potential of a relationship, in part, by evaluating what kind of change is or isn't taking place – in *you*. I'm not talking about emotions. I mean, who are you when you're with him? Who is he when he's with you? Who are each of you when you're in a group with others? Around each other's families? Do one or both of you change in different crowds? And is either of you being untrue to yourself in this relationship?

The type of change that occurs in me may change whether or not I proceed with a relationship. The *change* in me *changes* every dynamic of the relationship, either positively or negatively, and ultimately affects the overall health of the relationship.

Oftentimes, I need to seek input from someone close to me, like my mom or my sister, to help me identify changes that have occurred in me, because they can see things I can't see in myself. In fact, one of the main ways that my parents knew the guy I was dating a few years ago was not *the one* was by how I had changed throughout the relationship. I was no longer making rational decisions; I was acting in ways uncharacteristic of myself. I was not focusing on developing my dreams, gifts, and desires. Where I typically am a relatively stable individual, I had become an emotional basket-case, unstable and prone to outbursts of crying, fear, anger, and unbelief like I had never experienced before. Even I could tell that I had lost my confidence in who I was, and confidence was something I had never really struggled with before. Thank God for His Grace! When that relationship was over, I immediately felt free to be myself again! I am so much happier living life as single *me* than I ever was while dating and trying to be someone else.

If you hate who you've become in a dating relationship, it's time to get out of the relationship! Let's stop wasting time in relationships that are turning us into co-dependent, insecure, depressed, jealous, bitter, or even rebellious individuals. We're called to be Women of God, and God is Love. Let's make sure the relationship is reflecting Love in and through us as we've come to know Love in our journey together.

Truly healthy relationships will bear good fruit, positive changes, in both the man and the woman. If you find it easier to be yourself and if you *like* who you are becoming, that's a really good sign. If he drives you toward your dreams and goals, and if you spark hope and inspiration for his dreams and goals, that can all be really good! If you are both running toward God with all your hearts *before* you start dating, and then you *keep* running toward God with all your hearts while you're dating, that's another really good sign!

Pay attention to the changes, because change changes everything.

Key 7: Seek Godly Counsel.

This is one of the most important steps when you are considering a relationship, yet it is the one that is probably most often overlooked or bypassed. When you're connected to the Body of Christ (the Church), you have a wealth of protection available to you in the spiritual covering God has given you – your pastors and church leaders. Don't hesitate to go to them and ask them their input about the relationship, even *before* you embark in the relationship. I only wish I had listened to my pastors when they cautioned me not to date that particular guy. Even though he and I were both Christians actively pursuing God, our pastors could see things we couldn't see. They tried to warn me, and it wasn't what I wanted to hear. Now I see how I was in the wrong by ignoring their warnings. Unfortunately, I've seen far too many young adults do the same in the years since. It's too easy to suspect that your pastors want only to control you and keep you from happiness, but it's not that at all. Like loving parents, they want to protect you from the dangers they see ahead in the relationship. You would do well to heed their wise counsel!

Two sets of people I trusted most – my parents and my pastors – both cautioned me against that relationship. I thought I needed to prove that I could hear God for myself. That was a huge lesson learned, and it left me humbled and repentant. I only hope you will choose the wiser path!

> *Where no counsel is, the people fall: but in the multitude of counselors there is safety* (Proverbs 11:14 KJV).

Just remember that not everyone who has an opinion is qualified to be a "counselor" to you. Seek counsel from those who are established, trusted spiritual authorities in your life. In their counsel, you will find safety.

Key 8:   Remember that the types of signals you send can determine the type of man you attract.

We need to guard our own behavior and make sure that we aren't sending flippant, flirtatious signals, which would typically attract flippant, flirtatious guys. I used to wonder if something was wrong with me because I never had guys beating down my door or blowing up my phone. I finally realized that I was better off without that kind of attention, because most of the guys who were pursuing the flirtatious girls weren't the kind of guys I wanted to attract anyway.

I decided a long time ago to be intentional about *not* being a flirt. I recognized that perpetual flirts tend to attract men who are the same way, and these men often seem to have surface-level intentions; they aren't the men seeking a meaningful, lifelong commitment. I am now free from the pressure of trying to impress and attract every man I pass each day, because quite frankly, I don't *want* to attract most men!

As women, we have to realize that our charm and beauty are not intended to tease or control men. Rather, we should focus our efforts on controlling ourselves and guarding our hearts. You can send the flirty signals and play the mind-games; you can play hard-to-get, the damsel-in-distress, or the all-powerful, in-control feminist, but you will not attract a man of any substance or worth that way. **You will be the most attractive you can be when you are simply being true to who you really are!**

TRUSTING THE FATHER

These eight keys will help keep us on course as we keep our eyes open for *the one.* Even still, there are many unknowns in this season of Single, but do you know what I'm discovering? It's okay for me *not* to know all the answers! In fact, the beauty is often in the unfolding of the mystery. That's why most of us don't want to read the end of the book first or watch the end of the movie first. As tempting as it is to want to know the outcome now, we know we will miss out on the fullness of the experience if we jump ahead and find out too soon! Just remember, ultimately, God's best for us will come from God Himself. We don't have to make it happen. So let's keep our eyes fixed on our Father, trusting Him to lead us every step of the way.

Chapter Thirteen
FANTASY AND FAIRY TALES

MY STORY

Most of my life in Single can be traced from one fantasy to the next – elaborate crushes that, when put together end-to-end, make up all of my teen years and much of my adulthood so far. I've given you tidbits along the way, but allow me a few moments to share with you the overall picture of my journey in Single up until now – the journey that led me to writing this book.

For as long as I can remember, I have dreamed about finding *the one* and becoming a wife and eventually a mother. In the sixth grade, I began praying for my future husband. I prayed that God would keep him pure for me, and I prayed that God would keep me pure for him. Purity was and still is a big deal to me. Even as I made a determined commitment to God to keep my virginity until my wedding night, I still prayed for God's help in fulfilling that promise, because I didn't want to overestimate my own willpower and ability to follow through with the decision.

The focus of my life as a teenager always revolved around God and the house of God (my parents are pastors, so I've grown up immersed in church), but my desires for future companionship and marriage were forefront in my mind for as long as I can remember. In other words, like a lot of pre-teen and teenage girls, I was inclined toward being obsessed with silly crushes on boys all around me. And like many other girls, those silly crushes were all-too-serious in my own mind.

From the time I was 12 until I was 22, I lived in a cycle of what I call "marathon crushes;" I fell hard for guys I barely knew (and who barely knew I existed), but in each case, I was convinced he was *the one.* As grounded and stable as I was in other areas of my life, such as my faith and family, my ideas of romance and marriage were mostly rooted in sheer, unrealistic fantasy.

It may sound juvenile, but it was a seriously dangerous pattern that I fell into. I can literally mark that 10-year period of my life by who I thought I was in love with at each point along the way. It went something like this:

From 12 to 13 years old, I liked that one guy from church who sometimes talked to me. After that, it was that hugely successful, Christian recording artist, whom I just knew I would marry when I got old enough. That daydream ended at age 14 when the four-year marathon crush began.

That's right. My entire high school career included my solidified belief that this guy would fall in love with me and we would get married. It didn't matter that we'd only met a few times or that he wouldn't recognize me if he passed me on the street (which he would never have done, because we lived in entirely different states). From the time I was 14 until I was 18 years old, I simply knew he was *the one.* It was just a matter of time until he realized it (you know, after he figured out who I was and all). The fantasy was real to me.

As an 18-year-old in my first year on a college campus filled with new "prospects," I suddenly got over the out-of-state guy, and my interests bounced from one guy to another as I explored this new territory. Then came Summer Break when I was 19, and along with it came the *big one*.

This one didn't run a full four years as the previous crush had, but it was much deeper for me in how heavily I invested my emotions into this potential relationship. This is the one I gave my heart to more than any of the ones before. Just like the last guy, I didn't really know this guy when I decided he was worthy of my affections, and just like all the ones before, I never even dated him. But I gave him my heart, completely unbeknownst to him and completely regardless of whether or not he wanted it or was capable of caring for it.

From everything I could tell in the beginning, he seemed to be exactly what I wanted in my future husband. During the three-year lifetime of that very intense crush, which included a period of time in which I actually did get to know him and we became friends, I thought I was in love with him. In fact, at some points along the way, I truly believed that God had spoken to me and told me he was *the one* for me. That happened during those college years I told you about, when we girls were trying so hard to follow God but wanted so desperately to find our husbands. So for three years, this guy consumed my thoughts, my heart, and even my prayers. I was his forever if he wanted me. But as it turns out, he didn't.

When I first started getting to know him, I had already convinced myself that he was *the one,* so I quickly overlooked warning signs that he might not be everything I had imagined. At first, just as I had suspected, it seemed our gifts and callings lined up. He seemed to be almost everything I had asked God for on my "list." But as the months went by, I began to get the nagging feeling that this just wasn't God's best for me. By this point, though, I had invested so much time, energy, and emotion into him that I held on ever so tightly, because the thought of "starting over" was just too much to bear. Besides, I was convinced that he could still become everything I had built him up to be in my mind. So I prayed for him earnestly – I interceded for him, if you will. But my true motivation was that I still wanted God to let me have something I knew wasn't right – this relationship that was not crafted by God for me like I had originally thought it was.

The more we got to know each other, the more I found myself fighting the dreaded feeling that something wasn't right, even in our platonic friendship. I desperately clung to the hope that at some point, he would open his eyes and begin to cherish me as the gift from God that I wanted to be to him, but the more our friendship progressed, the more I realized he did not cherish me at all.

I shared with you earlier about the moment when Truth sank in, when my family and I were on vacation and my mother pointed out that his phone call to me was only about what interested him. My eyes were finally opened, causing me to realize that the pain of being unappreciated was greater than the pain of letting go.

One of my first evenings back in town after that vacation, I went home and had the most honest, gut-wrenching time with God that I had had in years. I was finally letting go after years of trying to convince both God and myself that this guy was *the one*. It was horribly painful. Freedom and failure battled it out that night, and I remember sitting on my bedroom floor, sobbing relentlessly, because I finally knew. I finally admitted that he was not *the one*, that I had been wrong about what I thought God had said to me about the relationship, and that I deserved somebody who would appreciate me and value me. Even though it hurt so deeply, that night was a night filled with hope and freedom.

Admitting I was wrong about hearing God's voice was hard, because my relationship with God is ultimately the center of my entire life. So being wrong didn't mean I was just wrong about this. It caused me to distrust my ability to hear God altogether, and the impact of that was actually more scary to me than the impact of letting go of the emotional connection to this guy. Nevertheless, at this point in my life, it was more important to free myself from the bondage of the gripping fantasy I had been clinging to than it was for me to be, well, *right*.

That night, it was okay that I had failed at hearing God, that I had failed by letting my emotions go to the wrong guy (again), and that I had failed at keeping God the number one priority (again). Why was it okay? Because the only way I was going to find freedom was in conceding failure – recognizing my inability to figure it all out or have it all under control, realizing the error of my ways, and asking God's forgiveness. Three years of holding my feelings just out of reach from God had taken their toll on me, and I was done fighting what I knew was right. I surrendered.

The freedom that met me that night was worth it. Of course, I had to walk out the process of allowing God to heal my heart from the rejection and the disappointment, but God *did* heal my heart. In fact, He gave me renewed hope with a clean slate to start dreaming again.

So after spending a good, solid 10 years of my youth in marathon crushes, God brought me to a place of resting in Him. The years of marathon crushes ended that night, once and for all, in a moment when I made myself vulnerable to the perfect Love of my Father God.

Over a year later, I entered into my first real dating relationship, the end of which I described in the introduction of this book. So technically, I was almost 24 when I had my first boyfriend. Some people gawk when I tell them that; however, believe it or not, I actually wish my first boyfriend hadn't even been then, because this was the relationship about which I ignored my parents' and my pastors' warnings. Thank God for His divine intervention! God saved both that guy and me from a horrible mistake, as we were already talking about marriage as soon as the relationship began. But I wasn't God's best for him, and he wasn't God's best for me. He broke up with me seven months later, and after the initial shock and subsequent recovery, I never looked back. That was that.

When I began writing this book, I had just passed my 26th birthday. At that time, a year and a half had already passed since the end of that relationship, and more time has passed from then until now. Let me pause and tell you, God is so awesome and so very faithful.

Two years earlier, I was planning to marry and spend the rest of my life with the wrong guy for me. Had our plans succeeded, I would be living in a different city, doing different things, existing in an entirely different way than I am right now. As it is, the time following that breakup has actually been wonderful. All-in-all, I have finally learned to live in a place of contentment and trust in God, a place I had longed for throughout Single but was never totally convinced was possible. For the first time since I can remember, I've been okay with not having any prospects on the horizon, even with the "biological clock" ticking past all those milestone ages when I thought I would have already been married.

I know that God knows my heart's desires. He knows that I want to be married at a relatively young age. He knows I've dreamed of having four kids some day, and He knows how to make that happen. **I just have to trust Him that time is not running out for my dreams to come true.** I've finally decided that it's got to be all Him making this thing happen; it's better for me just to enjoy the ride in the meantime!

FANTASY VS. FAITH

I've gone to much detail to share with you some very vulnerable pieces of my story, and I realize that some people might think I was a flighty, unstable person. Honestly, I know my story is different than a lot of people's, but if nothing else, I hope you can at least relate to it in the fact that we are both imperfect daughters who are loved by a Perfect Father.

Nonetheless, as the years have gone by, I've discovered that I'm not entirely alone in the trap I fell into. As Christian single women, we have these desires for God and for our future lives and ministries with our future husbands, but **it is so easy to confuse fantasy with faith.**

Maybe you're like me and have experienced this cycle first-hand. It's one thing to believe God for the impossible, to believe Him to fulfill your dreams and desires, and to believe Him to take care of your future. That's faith. It's another thing to pinpoint a man, outside of Wisdom and the keys we discussed in the previous chapter, and start trying to plug him into God's plan for your life. That's fantasy.

In all of the situations I shared with you, I thought I was walking in faith. It looked ridiculous. It sounded absurd. And it was! That's how I should have known that it was fantasy. Believing God to cause a man who had never met me to fall in love with me – that was definitely fantasy and not faith. Faith would have trusted God's plan and Wisdom for me; instead, my impatience bred fantasy in me that led my heart down some painful paths and completely set me up for rejection numerous times.

If you've been in similar situations, either as a teenager or as an adult, just remember that **Faith and Wisdom walk hand-in-hand.** Yes, there are times when Faith requires us to take a risk that leads us out of our comfort zones; there are other times when Wisdom will keep us from taking a leap that isn't quite right. But even still, Faith and Wisdom operate with one another, not against one another.

If I believed in regret, I would regret having gone down the path of fantasy, because I see now how unhealthy and dangerous it was, not to mention how overall unhappy I was while walking that path. However, I just can't totally believe in regret, even though there are things I sometimes wish I had used better common sense about. I just can't give regret a prominent place in my life. Let me share with you why I feel this way.

TURNING THE PAST INTO PURPOSE

Every circumstance of your past is being woven together with all of the other experiences in your life, along with your personality, intricacies, character, and preferences, in order to create the fabric of who you are. You may think that fabric can't possibly be beautiful, considering all you've been through.

The true beauty is that, no matter how ugly one strand of thread may seem to be when you look at it by itself, when it is incorporated into a life that is now surrendered to and made whole in God, it is a contributing factor to a wonderful piece of art – a masterpiece, in fact. Your life and your story are unique to you, and this is why I say I don't necessarily believe in regrets.

Do not despise your past, even though it was not ideal, but don't try to repeat it, either. From here on, look for God's protection in every area of your life, and be willing to accept it and stand under His guarding hand.

Whether you are happy with your choices up until now or not, let your past be what it is, and find your self-worth and fulfillment in your relationship with our Father, not in what your past was or could have been. God takes all that we have to offer Him and weaves it into the beauty of the destiny He created for us. That's why I can't really live with regret – because I know that my Father is big enough and creative enough to find a place for those less-than-beautiful threads and make them beautiful indeed as I walk with Him.

Before we leave this subject of fantasies and before we wrap up our journey together, I want us to tackle one more prevalent mindset that many of us deal with in our day. This is something I've been looking forward to sharing with you, but I've saved it until now to help us tie things up. I call it the modern-day fairy tale.

PRINCES AND PRINCESSES

I know the age-old, favorite fairy tales are of those when royalty falls in love with a pauper, and Prince Charming rescues the poor peasant, whisking her off to live in the palace, happily ever after.

I think that many of us, albeit subconsciously, have had that sort of expectation regarding our future husbands. On some level or another, we expect that our Prince Charming is going to have everything together and is going to swoop into our lives and whisk us off to a land of perfection in every way.

See, we overplay the "damsel in distress" scenario in our culture. We think that a man wants to come in and fix all of our imperfections. If I'm insecure, his confidence will rescue me from insecurity. If I'm financially unstable, he will come and swoop in with his already-established wealth and fix everything. If I'm spiritually weak, his strength will help me walk the straight and narrow without faltering. Whatever my glaring problems are, I just know that when he finds me, Happily Ever After will finally begin. I'll finally be complete.

Your Better Half

I just need to tell you this: You are so much more than a "better half" to someone. In fact, I hate that term, "better half." Do you know why? Because it implies that marriage is made up of two incomplete individuals. I believe the ideal, healthy marriage is made up of two already complete people, two people who know who they are in God. Sure, you will continue growing together, and of course, you will find ways to complete one another. Neither of you will be *completely perfect,* so I'm not suggesting that you have to have your act together in totality before you can get married. If that were the case, none of us would ever be ready to marry! We always have room to grow and improve and better ourselves. However, I do believe each of you should have a solid foundation as individuals, knowing who you are in God and having at least some sense of where God is taking you (the dreams and visions God has for your future).

Completely Incomplete

I'm not trying to destroy our romantic hopes for marriage here. It's just that we have romanticized the notion of being desperately incomplete until our spouse finds us and finally completes us, to the point that I think many of us are afraid to let God complete us, because we think that's our future husband's job. We've thought this was the recipe to the perfect union, when in fact, it is a recipe for disaster. **Two incomplete people will make a fragmented, incomplete marriage.**

We used the analogy early on about a $100 bill. Granted, we are worth so much more than money; however, to make my point, let's consider it again. Logic says that two halves make a whole. However, if you take a half of a $100 bill, how much is it worth? Is it worth $50? No, by itself, a half-bill is worthless. And if you try to piece it together with a half from a different $100 bill, it still doesn't make a whole; it makes two devalued halves, which together constitute a counterfeit. Each bill is marked with a distinct identity, and it cannot regain its own value unless it is complete in its original identity, given to it by its maker. Likewise, you can never be made complete by someone else. You were marked with a specific identity, an imprint made by your Creator, and you can never be complete by trying to unite with another incomplete person. If you try, you'll just be masquerading as a whole union – a complete marriage on the surface – but God is the only One who can complete your true identity. When two whole people come together, secure in who they are, they form one whole, dynamic union before God, and the power they have is increased exponentially! They become an unstoppable force in God's kingdom!

The Rescuer Standing in Front of You

Here's the problem with our "damsel in distress" approach to romance: **We're looking for a man to do what Jesus Christ has already done for us.**

Jesus has already come—He swooped down from heaven, if you will—and gave His entire life to rescue you! He's rescued you from sin, from insecurity, from fear, from lack, and from distress. So for you to keep playing the poor damsel waiting for your rescuer is for you to ignore and reject the all-encompassing Love He has already offered you!

If you can't be made complete in Jesus' Love for you, how will you ever be made complete in the love offered you by a mere, mortal man? And how can you ever offer your husband a complete love? The answer is that you won't be able to do either.

A man cannot do for you what only Jesus can. A man cannot be perfection for you; only Jesus can be that.

We've got to stop playing fairy tales with our futures. A truly confident man of God isn't looking for a woman to rescue. He is looking for a woman who has already been rescued by the Love of God, so that together, they can join forces and go out and rescue others for the sake of the Kingdom and righteousness.

It's time for us to stop playing the damsel in distress, stop waiting around for a man to come fix all our problems, and stop expecting a man to be more than he is capable of being. It's time for us to rise up and allow God to shape us in order to make us the women of God He called us to be! **It's time for us to realize that, because of what Jesus has done for us, Happily Ever After has already begun.**

The Kingdom's Favorite Princess

Let's not stop there. Knowing that we are indeed daughters of the King, let's ask ourselves the tough question: Are we making ourselves valuable in the Kingdom of our Father?

If you like a good fairy tale, then you know that nobody ever likes the self-centered princess. But the kingdom loves and celebrates the selfless, humble, down-to-earth princess who serves and loves everyone in her father's kingdom. Well, guess what? If your Father is the King – the King of all kings, actually – then that makes you a princess. So while you're waiting around for Prince Charming to come rescue you (from what, the palace of the greatest King ever?), what are you doing to learn the heart of your Father and to serve His people?

If you want to marry a prince, stop trying to be Cinderella, and start being the princess you already are.

Don't minimize your callings and gifts to being effective only when another human being enters the picture and becomes your spouse. God has greatness for you in Single, but you'll never find it if you're only looking inward.

I challenge you to turn your focus outward. Many of our prayers are answered when we take our eyes off of ourselves and focus on the Father and on serving others. Let's make a point to thank God for this gift of Single, and let's ask Him to show us what it is that He wants us to do with this very good gift He has given us.

To do that, we *must* dream beyond what we can see right now. We must allow the Holy Spirit to breathe into our imaginations and our desires and give us dreams for the future, in spite of all the major unknowns staring us in the face. We have to realize that He is the Master Planner, and we cannot out-dream Him or mess up His plans for our lives by dreaming bigger than we have so far. We must keep dreaming.

So that's easy for me to tell you to do. But now that we've confronted and dispelled the fantasies and the fairy tales, what about our dreams – you know, the ones actually rooted in Faith and trust in our Father's good intentions for us? What do those dreams look like?

KEEP DREAMING

In light of our new perspective, here's my dream. I dream for a man who will love me and cherish me, a man who knows who he is in God. He has prepared himself to be a true husband, just as I am preparing to be a true wife. He will be a visionary - never satisfied with average. He will be a doer, not just a big talker. He will be transparent with me and will not be afraid of my seeing his weaknesses. On the other hand, he will not despise my weaknesses; neither will he be intimidated by my strengths. He will be a man strong in character and integrity but tender toward the things of God.

Will he be perfect? No. But he will be perfect for me, and although I am not perfect, either, I will be perfect for him!

So what about you, dear friend? Now that you know it's actually possible for us to dream the Faith-kind of dreams without slipping into the dangerous slope of fantasies and fairy tales, what is it that you see? When you look at your future through the loving eyes of our Father, the King, what is your dream?

Keep dreaming, beloved Princess. Keep dreaming.

Epilogue
WORTH WAITING FOR

As I begin the conclusion of this book, now almost a full seven months after I started writing the very first thoughts, I have already begun to see shifting in my season of Single. When I began writing this book, I was here in my hometown, a small city by most standards; I was extremely active in my church, which right now is considered to be a small church by some; I was being faithful at my job; and I was living life praying for my future husband but having absolutely *no* idea where he was going to come from!

When I was eighteen, I actually moved away from this city, convinced that whoever my husband was, I would not find him here! My mother told me time after time, "Amy, if you are supposed to be here, God will help your husband find you, no matter where he is." Although I knew what she said was true, it seemed highly unlikely. So I went to college out-of-state – a breeding ground for eligible bachelors, one would think – and then I lived on my own for several years in Nashville, a much larger city than where I was raised, only to find out that my husband was in neither of those places.

SWNP: THE PLAIN OF IMPATIENCE

I was Single-With-No-Prospects, living in what I call the "*plain of impatience*" – you know, like a piece of flat land where you can see for miles in every direction, but there are absolutely *no* possibilities on the horizon.

In that plain, I discovered that impatience is a powerful force when it goes unchecked in our lives. It can drive us to making rash decisions, like moving away from where we are grounded and growing, because we're convinced there are no options where we are. That can be a city, like I thought, or it can be a life-giving church that you leave in order to seek greener pastures. Impatience can cause us to choose one college over another or turn down one job for a different one, all in the pursuit of viable "prospects."

Ultimately, **impatience breeds compromise, and compromise breeds catastrophe** in our lives, either physically, mentally, emotionally, spiritually, or all of the above. That edge of catastrophe is what eventually brought me back to where I was supposed to be – my home church in my hometown. A series of mind-boggling events filled with turmoil left me no choice but to return home where I belonged, in spite of my lack of expectation for finding a husband here.

WAITING & TRUSTING

"Waiting patiently." What an oxymoron, huh? When it comes to something as important as meeting our lifelong spouse, waiting patiently seems completely impossible. And it is impossible, except for one thing: Trust. **Trust makes waiting patiently possible.** I offer you encouragement from the Apostle Paul's words:

> *...for I know the one in whom I **trust**, and I am sure that **he is able to guard what I have entrusted to him** until the day of his return* (2 Timothy 1:12 NLT).

Trust is the key to overcoming impatience.

I've tried to illustrate this to you throughout my own story so far, but now – as I'm nearing the conclusion of this book – I actually have much more of the story I can share with you!

THE BEGINNING

Picking up my story where we left off, here I was back in my hometown when I began writing this book. I had finally found that wonderful season of contentment, and my general outlook toward Single could have been described as: *Well, God, I have no idea where he is going to come from, but I am going to keep myself where You want me to be, and I'm going to trust You to bring us together at the right time, in the right place.*

Basically, I was at a point of: *I give up trying on my own. You were right all along. Jesus, take over.*

A little over two months ago, a friend of mine from out of town called me. Our families have been friends for many, many years, but living 700 miles apart, I had not seen or spoken to him in about seven years (remember, I'd been off at college and living in Nashville, so even when our families did hear from each other, I wasn't around to be part of it). We simply had been living our lives all this time and had not had opportunity to "touch base" in quite a while; in fact, the last time I had seen him, I was about 18 or 19 years old. This was a boy whom I was always fond of but had never really considered as more than a friend.

So he called me recently, completely unexpected, breaking the unintentional seven-year silence between us. We immediately reconnected on the phone that night from Missouri to Virginia, and we began rebuilding our friendship – this time on more genuine levels than we ever had opportunity to do before. He continued calling me, and over the six weeks that followed, we spent a lot of time getting to know each other through conversations, learning about each other's ideals and dreams and expectations out of life. As it turns out, his dad was coming out here to speak at our church, so he decided to come along; it was the first time we had seen each other since we were both teenagers. It didn't take long after that until we began exploring the possibility of a dating relationship.

As I write to you now, we are dating long-distance, and I am praying about whether or not he could, maybe, possibly be *the one* for me. It seems a little far-fetched still, with so much distance between us, and it seems like a crazy notion; this all just happened out of nowhere! So we shall see...

THE JOURNEY CONTINUES

I'm about to tell you something that you might find unbelievable, so please brace yourself. While seven months passed from the time I penned the first word of this book until I began writing this epilogue, a lot more time has passed since then. A *whole lot* of time. Ten and a half years have gone by since I began writing to you!

Now, let me say, I never dreamed it would take me this long to finish this book, and I don't use life circumstances as an excuse for putting it on the back burner for so long (okay, maybe more like packing it in a box and sticking it in the attic). But in a way, I'm glad I didn't finish writing to you before now, because now I get to tell you the rest of the story. Now I get to tell you how all the things we've struggled with in Single are going to be okay. I get to tell you that God's faithfulness is real, and that He really will reward our patience and trust – that He really does give good gifts to His children.

So now for the rest of the story...

As it turns out, that crazy, out-of-the-blue reconnection on the phone led to a whirlwind of a dating process, a marriage proposal, his moving all the way from St. Louis to Roanoke, and our getting married just one year after we began dating. As it turns out, that cute little kid from my childhood was and is my *one*.

Now I'm no longer writing to you as a 26-year-old single. In fact, I've spent much of the last few months going through this book, preserving the raw feelings and insights I had as that 26-year-old, but inserting new aspects of Wisdom and understanding I have gained over the past ten years – things I would have liked to have known better back then. I wanted to offer you the opportunity to relate to me as the woman who began writing this book – the woman who knows first-hand how challenging Single can be – but now I offer you the opportunity of finding hope from the path that has unfolded for the woman I have become.

I told you in the beginning that I began writing this book as a sort of offering to God, a way to let God use my season of Single however He saw fit. I had no idea when I began typing the first words that my *one* would enter my life just five months later, and that only a year and a half after starting this book, I would exit Single forever. How much more appreciative I am now of the contentment He brought me before He offered me the next gift He had planned!

WORTH THE WAIT

As I sit here filling you in on the details, I am now 36 years old, and I have three of the most beautiful blessings in the world running around here calling me "Mommy." Do you remember my sharing with you that I always desired to get married and have four kids? Well, as I put the finishing touches on this book, I'm due to deliver our fourth child about five weeks from now. It is such a blessing to me to realize that, even though it seemed like my dreams were getting further and further away, and even though I was so worried about how old I was and whether or not I'd have time for these dreams to come to pass, God swooped in and made it all happen in exactly His timing! I imagine He was probably smiling knowingly at me the entire time that I was busy stressing about how it would all happen.

So I'm sure you're asking, *Did you get your knight in shining armor? Was it worth the wait?* The short answer is yes and YES! But of course, I won't leave you with only the short answer.

First, I have learned that God does sometimes surprise us. Tim didn't come the way I expected, and he caught me off-guard in some ways. He didn't even entirely match my long, particular "list" that I had made years before. But he did match the core values, the non-negotiables, the things we talked about in

Chapter Twelve. The things that really mattered were spot-on. I fell in love with Tim, because he quickly became my best friend, and he treated me like a queen. He didn't keep me around just to meet his need for companionship. He didn't call only when he had nothing better to do. He made me a priority, and he went out of his way to make sure I knew he valued me. The first time he flew out here to see me once we were dating, he actually packed a dozen red roses in his luggage and brought them on the plane, so he could give them to me after he arrived! I'm not sure what's more impressive, the fact that he thought to do that or the miracle that the roses didn't get damaged in transit; either way, I was pretty impressed! But I didn't just fall in love with how he treated me; those were just clues to the character he carried on the inside. I truly love the man that he is.

Tim loves God. He was raised in a family that instilled godly character, morals, and principles in him. He is respectful and considerate, and he is responsible and trustworthy. Tim has proven to be a wonderful, loving husband and father; he cares about me emotionally, spiritually, mentally, physically, and financially. He puts the children and me before himself, almost to a fault at times, and he strives to make sure our family is close-knit and well-provided for.

There's one particular thing I want to share with you, simply because I mentioned it earlier on in our journey, and I want you to know what God did. When God gave me Tim, He gave me one very important thing I had asked for since I was in the sixth grade. I shared with you earlier that I had made a commitment to keep myself sexually pure until marriage, and I had asked God to keep my husband pure until marriage, too. I can't even begin to describe how huge of a blessing and reward it was that when we met each other at the altar for our wedding, neither of us had ever given ourselves sexually to anyone else. I share this, because I want you to know that purity is possible! God will empower you from this day forward to carry out the commitments you've made to Him, and you will be so genuinely thankful that you never compromised those commitments.

THE JOURNEY SINCE THEN

To keep us grounded in reality, I want to be transparent with you. When they say marriage is hard work, they are right! We are going to celebrate our tenth anniversary later this year, but I will be honest and say that it has not all been easy. As awesome as Tim is, he isn't perfect, and as it turns out, neither am I. We've each learned a lot about ourselves and about one another, and we've had to work through some pretty serious misunderstandings along the way. We've had some bumpy patches, and we've even had a few seasons when I wondered how we would ever get through to the other side. Had it not been for the Grace of God, we might have thrown in the towel and given up. Even with God's divine hand on our lives and marriage, we have learned that Love really is a decision, a commitment. We have made the choice to stay committed to one another even when it didn't feel like the most pleasant thing to do, and as a result, God has helped us through the tough times.

Of course, this isn't a book about marriage; I just want you to be prepared so that when you and your *one* get married, and when the butterflies go away and reality hits, you don't think you've missed God! Stay committed to God, and once you and your husband have entered into marriage covenant together, stay committed to one another, no matter what. God's faithfulness will see you through.

ENJOY THE JOURNEY

My story probably doesn't look exactly like yours, and yours won't look exactly like the next person's. But I can say with confidence that if you trust God and keep your eyes on Him, stay in His Word, and listen to the wise counsel of the spiritual leaders He has put in your life, you absolutely *will* navigate your season of Single successfully!

Remember, it's not so much about what season you're in; it's about staying on the right path while you're in it, appreciating the gifts God has given, and keeping yourself safely tucked away in the protection and covering of your Father's Love for you.

God has so much good in store for you. Trust the Love of our Father, stay safe in His shadow, and don't forget to enjoy the journey.

I pray for every one of you, and with all my heart, I thank you for allowing me to be part of your story of Single.

Blessings to you,

Amy

FOOTNOTES

Chapter Seven
1. lexiconcordance.com, Hebrew word H5414
2. lexiconcordance.com, Greek word G1939
3. lexiconcordance.com, Hebrew word H4862

ABOUT THE AUTHOR

Amy Smith is the Worship Pastor of Church Alive International in Roanoke, Virginia. The church was pioneered by her family when she was 13 years old, so she has served in a plethora of ministry areas, from church janitor to children's teacher, from administration to music and media.

Growing up in ministry with her parents and family, Amy has a deep love for the Church and for helping people relate to God in real, personal ways. As a women's small group leader and former youth leader, she is particularly passionate about inspiring single women and young ladies to discover their value and purpose in God's eyes and to choose purity and integrity over the cheapened forms of romance and affirmation offered in our society today.

Amy is a graduate of Lee University in Cleveland, Tennessee, and she spent almost three years in Nashville, Tennessee, before returning to her home and church in Roanoke in 2003. Next to her relationship with God, her family is the most important part of her life, so she finds it both rewarding and fulfilling to serve together with them in ministry.

Write the author at:

Amy Smith
Church Alive International
PO Box 12346
Roanoke, VA 24024

Follow the Softer Side of Single's blog at
churchaliveintl.com/blog.